POWER
FROM ON
HIGH

POWER
FROM ON
HIGH

C. MAX CALDWELL

Covenant Communications, Inc.

Published by Covenant Communications, Inc.
American Fork, Utah

Printed in Canada
First Printing: September 2008

15 14 13 12 11 10 09 08   10 9 8 7 6 5 4 3 2 1

ISBN 13: 978-1-59811-659-5
ISBN 10: 1-59811-659-2

ACKNOWLEDGMENTS

I express sincere gratitude to Shauna Humphreys for her insightful competence, her gracious way of making suggestions, and her editorial expertise. I have also greatly appreciated Kathryn Jenkins for her encouragement and patient persuasions. May other associates have likewise served as mentors over the years while sharing their knowledge and understanding, thus contributing to my ongoing learning experience.

I express deep thanks and gratitude to my wife, Joann, for her encouragement, assistance, and support throughout the preparation and completion of this work. During her life she has applied the principles and obtained the blessings discussed in this book. She is an example of one who has sought for, relied upon, and been sustained by power from on high.

Finally, I acknowledge my indebtedness to the Lord for my opportunities to serve in His Church and learn from Him and fellow workers many eternal truths upon which this book is based.

KEY TO ABBREVIATIONS

CR	Conference Report
CHMR	*Church History and Modern Revelation*
DNTC	*Doctrinal New Testament Commentary*
HC	*History of the Church*
TPJS	*Teachings of the Prophet Joseph Smith*
JD	*Journal of Discourses*

TABLE OF CONTENTS

INTRODUCTION

When my oldest son was four years old, I took him on a five-day fishing trip with my father and brother. His mother had expressed the usual motherly concerns when he asked to go, but hesitatingly yielded to his pleas to make the trip. Her anxieties would later prove to be justified. We drove my father's pickup truck to a beautiful spot in the Uinta Mountains, where we set up camp in an abandoned cabin that must have seen better days. Nonetheless, we greatly enjoyed our delightful paradisiacal retreat among the pines and lakes. After several delightful days, we left our Edenic garden, longing to remain, but content that we had accumulated treasured memories of many enjoyable moments. However, one incident that would prove to be most memorable was yet to occur.

Whenever my father drove his truck into remote areas he took a fifty-gallon, gasoline-filled barrel that he could use to refill the vehicle's fuel tank if and when that became necessary. This trip was no exception.

While we were enjoying our explorations that week, we used most of the fuel in the truck's tank, and so before leaving our "adopted cabin," we replenished the tank from the barrel and started down the mountain. We had gone only a short distance when the engine quit and the truck came to a stop. Though we tried everything we knew to get it running, every effort to start the engine again was a failure. It simply would not start.

Though the weather was not stormy at the moment, it had snowed that morning, and the air was cold. Temperatures continued to drop as the sun also dropped closer to sunset and darkness. Worse, we had no way of making contact with anyone to alert them to our stranded condition, and it was a long way to the closest known location where we might expect to find help.

We made a fire and gathered around it to keep warm, and we ate a little of the food we had left over. Spending the night out in the open under increasingly colder conditions was not a pleasant prospect, especially with my little four-year-old son and my father, whose body was trembling in the cold due to a weakened physical condition. By this time it was dark. Though we had previously done so, we prayed again most earnestly for heavenly help. We then remembered having passed a logging camp on the way up the mountain, and we sent my brother farther down the road to see if there might be anyone in that area. He returned later with the report that it was deserted; he could find no one. We did not know what to do next.

Sometime near midnight, we heard the sound of an approaching vehicle. Soon we saw lights flashing through the trees, and within minutes a familiar pickup truck pulled up next to our stalled vehicle. Emerging from the truck was a familiar form and voice asking why we had decided to spend the night there! It was my father's brother, Hugh. We were so relieved and grateful to see him. As a boy growing up, I had enjoyed many opportunities to spend time with Uncle Hugh, but never had I been as thrilled to be in his presence as I was at that moment.

After we explained our problem, we asked him why he was up there on the mountain in the middle of the night. He explained that he knew where we had gone and also knew we planned to return by Saturday night. That afternoon, he called to see how our trip had gone and learned from my mother we had not returned. He waited awhile, thinking we would arrive soon, but when we did not, he determined to come looking for us. Wisely, he had brought a tow chain and other tools that might be needed.

The chain was hooked to both vehicles, and he pulled us home. I drove the disabled truck without power steering, power brakes, headlights, or heater. It was a long journey that culminated in our safe arrival home as the morning sun was rising behind the hills, ending a miserable but most memorable night.

On Monday, we towed the truck to a repairman to learn the cause of our problem. He discovered that the fuel line was filled with liquid, but it was mostly water. We could only conclude that before we left home, someone must have siphoned out most of the fuel from our barrel and replaced it with water, resulting in extensive and expensive repairs to the vehicle.

I have often thought of that incident and the accompanying subtle principles embodied in it. The most important lesson for me came when we stood looking at a vehicle that appeared the same as it had when it was transporting us only moments earlier. It appeared to be as useful and capable as ever. Outwardly, it looked fine. But though it was still equipped with all of the essential systems and component parts, it was not capable of producing the power necessary to accomplish its designed tasks. The startling truth was that the flammable fluid needed to ignite the powerful engine had been irreversibly infiltrated. The impure fluid was hidden from visible detection by encasing tubes and metal chambers so that its disabling presence was undetected until it was too late to prevent damage. The once-powerful vehicle could not function.

After we were immobilized, we were helpless to change our status and were completely dependent on help from another source. Our greatest anxiety, being stranded in that remote area, concerned the possible inability of a little boy and his grandfather to survive the effects of our circumstances and the weather conditions surrounding us. I thought then, and often since, how much our situation was like our mortal lives wherein we cannot, by ourselves, rise above our fallen circumstances. We have not the power to overcome and transcend our mortal limitations. So we must turn to the Lord for help. Sometimes He answers prayers and fulfills our needs through the instrumentality of others. He did for us. An awareness of our plans and our delayed return home, coupled with a willingness to render service, though inconvenient for him, made it possible for my uncle to rescue us from our temporal trials that night. He became a savior for us when no other help was available. An automobile mechanic filled another vital role the following week as he repaired the internal damage within the vehicle's power plant.

This whole experience symbolized for me the dependence of mankind on the saving and redeeming power of the Savior. His atoning sacrifice and Resurrection not only saves us from permanent physical disabilities, but He also repairs internal spiritual damages incurred when we fail to follow narrow but straight paths leading toward home. This He does through His redeeming powers.

Unfortunately, many of us experience spiritual disasters. Everyone knows a mechanical engine cannot operate with water in the fuel lines. But we may presume there is no harm being done when we ingest spiritually impure ingredients into our personal power systems. We sometimes permit infiltration of impurities, such as dishonesty; suggestions of immorality embedded in music, clothing fashions, or entertaining stories; or even presentations of erotic behavior on screen or stage that encourages us to satisfy unbridled passions. Or we may fail to faithfully fulfill covenant responsibilities, resulting in a lowering level of our spiritual reservoirs.

Through all of this we may assume no harm is being done simply because we do not detect the gradual deterioration and damage. Such an assumption precipitates a disregard for prophetic warnings and causes the igniting power of the Holy Spirit to be diminished within us. Eventually it is stilled, resulting in a spiritual burnout with the accompanying inability to overcome the immobilizing power of the evil one. We may outwardly appear to be the same as when we had power to resist temptation, but inwardly, a leeching of precious spiritual power has silently been taking place. The Savior said that the ". . . wicked one cometh and taketh away light and truth [spiritual power], through disobedience, from the children of men . . ." and that we should "pray always lest that wicked one have power in you, and remove you out of your place" (D&C 93:39, 49).

Yielding to satanic influence in any degree results in the consequential loss of spiritual power, the replacement of which requires the repairing, saving, and healing power of the Savior's Atonement. Only through Jesus Christ and our adherence to our Father's plan of salvation can sufficient power be instilled within us to return to our heavenly home. Even though there are inherent challenges, including trials, inconveniences, and afflictions, His way provides our only hope.

The purpose for writing this book is to identify some of the gospel teachings that, when understood and applied, provide the individual with an increasing reservoir of spiritual power. Each of the ensuing chapters will present doctrinal discussions of restored gospel principles and practices that provide us with a connecting line to the Lord's power plant.

The Lord declared, "All things unto me are spiritual, and not at any time have I given unto you a law which was temporal" (D&C

29:34). Acquisition of spiritual power is predicated upon obedience to spiritual laws (see D&C 130:19–21). Blessed is the seeker and recipient of power from on high.

CHAPTER 1
ENDOWED WITH POWER FROM ON HIGH

In December 1830 the Lord gave a commandment "unto the church, that it is expedient in me that they should assemble together at the Ohio" (D&C 37:3). We should think what that announcement might have meant to some of those people, many of whom were living in scattered locations throughout upstate New York. Could there have been some who had only recently been working to clear land, build a home and fences, or establish a business or profession? Could there have been some who were in poor health or in a state of poverty or without means to make a move from their current location? Could there have been some who were taking care of aged parents or other kin and were the only caregivers available to those in need? Could there have been some who had infants or little children and were hesitant to move in winter conditions and attempt to settle in a place they had never seen before? Undoubtedly, there could have been a lot of unanswered questions.

The Lord surely knew their concerns and anxieties, because on January 2, 1831, He gave another revelation that began with His reminding them who it was that was asking them to go. He was not just another person with an idea. He was the God of Israel in Old Testament times. He was the Creator of the world in the cosmic space of the universe. He knows and sees all things. He had taken Enoch's city Zion from the earth and placed the wicked in chains of darkness. He assured the Saints that He was in their midst and had His eyes upon them (see D&C 38:1–7). He then told them some of the reasons they were being asked to gather in Ohio. They needed to leave to escape their enemies, and they were promised that if they would go, He would give them His law and *they would be endowed with power from on high* (see D&C 38:28–32). Only with the passage of time would they realize how far-reaching and magnificent that endowment of power would be.

Commonly, when Church members hear the words "endowed" or "endowment" they think of priesthood ordinances that are provided in the temples of the Lord. It is certainly a valid way to conceptualize the terms, and, in fact, it would become a part of the way the Lord would fulfill His promise. But there would be other dimensions of an endowment as well. So, how else was the Church in Ohio provided with power from on high? We will review some of the ways the divine promise was fulfilled. But before doing so, we should be aware that when the Lord speaks of the Church, He might be using the term in one or both of two different ways. First, the Church is an institution or organization that was officially and formally established April 6, 1830, in Fayette, New York. Secondly, the Lord said, "Whosoever repenteth and cometh unto me, the same is my church" (D&C 10:67). He might refer to either the institution or to worthy members as His church.

DOCTRINAL ENDOWMENT

The Ohio period of Church history was the most prolific of all time periods for the unfolding of revealed doctrines and teachings of the Lord. Of the 138 revelations published in the Doctrine and Covenants, 65 were received in Ohio. It was also in Ohio that Joseph Smith did most of his work of translating the Bible. His involvement in that assignment not only produced a great amount of information resulting in changes being made to biblical texts, but when Joseph made inquiry of textual meanings, he was often the recipient of additional revelation on the subject in question. A great number of revealed truths contained in the Doctrine and Covenants were a result of or in connection with his asking for divine insight while translating the Bible. It was also in Ohio that Joseph obtained the papyrus from the Egyptian mummies, which contained original writings of Abraham and Joseph from ancient times (see *HC,* 2:236), some of which was translated and published in the Pearl of Great Price.

When the Lord authorized the publication of the revelations contained in our Doctrine and Covenants, he made it possible for all His people to be endowed with the power of those revelations. The first two editions of that growing compilation were published in Ohio. Being endowed with power from the scriptural canon of the Church becomes apparent as one grasps the content and then experiences personal application of the doctrines contained in the gospel revelations. We remember also that the early Saints came from a background of mostly Protestant doctrine and were infants in the Restored Church as far as revealed gospel knowledge went. They had not been exposed to very much of the doctrinal revelations that had come and would yet be forthcoming from the heavens. It was a giant step upward for them to learn and live the sacred truths being revealed in this dispensation.

For example, consider the power of Section 76 of the Doctrine and Covenants, which contains much of the Lord's plan of salvation for His children and which was unfolded to a people trying to survive a spiritual famine in a barren theological desert. In this revelation we gain knowledge from six separate visions given to Joseph Smith and Sidney Rigdon in Hiram, Ohio. The first of those was a vision of the Savior, after which they testified of the living reality of Christ, substantiated in part by having seen Him. Knowing that He lives is a source of great power for all of us. We must know that He lives before His teachings will be of any value to us. On that fundamental truth we base our faith in Him as the first of all gospel principles.

From those six visions, we also discover that our response to a testimony of Jesus is the prime factor that determines our eventual and eternal destiny. Having that critical knowledge provides powerful motivation for us to obtain and be faithful to a personal assurance of the divinity and reality of Christ. Once that testimony is received, we then have an increased desire and capacity to be true to what we know, and thus become his witnesses as well as claimants upon His eternal promises and presence.

Organizational Endowment

In a revelation given on or about the day the Church was organized, the Lord refers to "the rise of the Church of Christ in these last days" (D&C 20:1). From an official membership of six members, the Church grew in numbers and likewise began to expand organizationally to meet the growing needs of its members. In the Ohio period, many Church offices were created in the organizational framework. It was in Ohio that the First Presidency was formed, the Quorums of Twelve and Seventy were established, the first stake and high council was organized, and the first bishop and first patriarch were called. The Prophet Joseph was shown the organizational order of the Church in vision and apparently saw some of the brethren who would be involved (see *HC,* 2:181–82, notes).

As part of the rise of the Church organization, Joseph called a meeting of the members of Zion's camp who had journeyed the previous year to Missouri. The meeting was held February 14, 1835, and was the one in which the Twelve Apostles were chosen and called. In that meeting, the Prophet Joseph made the following statement: "The weak things, even the smallest and weakest among us, shall be powerful and mighty, and great things shall be accomplished by you from this hour; and you shall begin to feel the whisperings of the Spirit of God; and the work of God shall begin to break forth from this time; and *you shall be endowed with power from on high* (*HC*, 2:182; emphasis added).

As the brethren received the mantle of their new callings, they began to function under the direction and with the power of the Lord through His Holy Spirit. They grew in wisdom and faith and learned the processes of inspiration while serving with faithful dedication. Their value to the people paralleled their value to the Lord as He continued to assist and lead the Saints, through their priesthood leaders, to grow spiritually stronger in their newly found status as members of the Kingdom of God.

In today's Church, we see the power and strength that is still inherent in the priesthood offices and the brethren who occupy them. It would be difficult to imagine the Church without the organization presently in existence. Our people depend upon inspired leadership and teachings that come through the Apostles and prophets and other General Authorities who serve in the leading councils of the Church. Those priesthood leaders are empowered and directed by the Lord to "build up the church, and regulate all the affairs of the same in all nations, first unto the Gentiles and secondly unto the Jews" (D&C 107:33–34).

There are other ways Saints across the world are endowed with spiritual power through the offices and organization of the Church. For example, they look to and are strengthened by the personal blessings that are revealed to and declared by ordained and inspired patriarchs. Additionally, callings and counsel are extended to the Church membership by inspired bishops as well as district, stake, and mission priesthood leaders, making it possible for the members to grow in faith and increase in spirituality through their own service while applying and following the directions they receive.

I recall interviewing a young man who was serving as a full-time missionary. He had been unfaithful to his covenants before being called to his mission and eventually confessed his unworthiness to his mission president. I was asked to visit with him to determine what should be done to resolve the matter. In our discussion, he described the situation, and then expressed the hope that his confession to me would clear the way for him to remain in his mission and continue his service there.

I remember posing a question to him as to whether he was unworthy at the time of his interview with his bishop. He admitted being untruthful in his responses to the questions of his bishop. I reminded him that he had placed his bishop in the position of being responsible to make recommendations in his behalf that were based on false representations resulting in the young man being responsible not only for his sins against the Lord, but also for having lied to the Lord's bishop.

As I spoke those words the young man's face reflected a new concern as he said in a trembling voice, "Do I have to talk about this with my bishop?" I said to him, "No, you don't have to talk with your bishop. You get to. Your bishop is your best friend in the Church. He is the one that can help you the most. He loves you and is anxious to do for you whatever is necessary for you to reestablish your worthiness before the Lord. His counsel to you will be the Lord's counsel, and you will be blessed as you follow and apply it." Fortunately, the young man willingly returned to the safe paths pointed out by his bishop and ultimately regained the peace of righteous doing.

Through the Church organizational structure of leaders, teachers, and all who faithfully serve in the Lord's kingdom, the Saints have been and are yet truly endowed with power from on high.

ENDOWMENT OF A TEMPLE

In December 1832, the Lord revealed the need for the Saints to establish, or build, "a house of God" (D&C 88:119). About five months later (June 1, 1833), the Lord chastised the elders of the Church for their delay in building the Lord's house (see D&C 95). However, the Lord reaffirmed His commandment for the house to be built and said, "In the which house I design to endow those whom I have chosen with power from on high" (D&C 95:8). Elder Joseph Fielding Smith observed the following:

> The elders of the Church, it would appear, had not taken this command seriously, presumably it had been overlooked in the consideration of so many wonderful things in that particular revelation [D&C 88]. . . . The Kirtland Temple was necessary before the apostles (who had not yet been called), and other elders of the Church could receive the endowment which the Lord had in store for them. The elders had been out preaching the Gospel and crying repentance ever since the Church was organized and many great men had heard and embraced the truth, nevertheless elders could not go forth in the power and authority which the Lord intended them to possess until this Temple was built where he could restore keys and powers essential to the more complete preaching of the Gospel and the administering in its ordinances (*CHMR*, 2:166–67).

The Lord did provide special priesthood ordinances as an endowment in the temple. But there was also a limitation as to how much was to be given in that first temple in Kirtland. President Brigham Young recounted that the

> . . . first Elders who helped to build it [Kirtland Temple] received a portion of their first endowments, or we might say more clearly, some of the first, or introductory, or initiatory ordinances, preparatory to an endowment.
>
> The preparatory ordinances there administered, though accompanied by the ministration of angels, and the presence of the Lord Jesus, were but a faint similitude of the ordinances of the House of the Lord in their fulness.
>
> [Speaking then of the full endowment, President Young defined it:] Your *endowment* is, to receive all those ordinances in the House of the Lord, which are necessary for you, after you have departed this life, to enable you to walk back to the presence of the Father, passing the angels who stand as sentinels, being enabled to give them the key words, the signs and tokens, pertaining to the Holy Priesthood, and gain your eternal exaltation in spite of earth and hell (*JD,* 2:31).

Only the Lord could endow a mortal person with sufficient power to realize and experience the blessings described by President Young. Without divine direction revealed through the channels chosen by the Lord, no mortal could possibly possess the knowledge or develop the capacity to enter a state of eternal exaltation. Without the bestowal of heavenly powers, it would be eternally impossible for anyone to transcend the limitations of mortality and transfer to the environments of the gods. But with the endowment of power provided in the temples of the Lord, the Father's children who honor their sacred covenants are assured of the obtaining of every blessing pronounced and promised in the priesthood ordinances of the temple.

In a meeting with the Council of the Twelve about four months before the dedication of the temple, the Prophet Joseph Smith gave the following admonition to the brethren:

> The endowment you are so anxious about, you cannot comprehend now, . . . but strive to be prepared in your hearts, be faithful in all things, that when we meet in the solemn assembly, . . . we must be clean every whit. . . . Do not watch for iniquity in each other, if you do you will not get an endowment, for God will not bestow it on such. But if we are faithful, and live by every word that proceeds forth from the mouth of God, I will venture to prophesy that we shall get a blessing that will be worth remembering. . . .
>
> You need an endowment, brethren, in order that you may be prepared and able to overcome all things (*HC*, 2:309).

It appears from the Prophet's admonition above, that the expected endowment would consist of more than ordinances. Inferred in the promised experience is a suggestion that there would also be a spiritual outpouring to edify and strengthen the attending brethren. Such expectation would be consistent with the prayed-for blessing mentioned in the revealed prayer of dedication "that all people who shall enter upon the threshold of the Lord's house may *feel thy power,* and feel constrained to acknowledge that thou hast sanctified it, and that it is thy house, a place of thy holiness" (D&C 109:13; emphasis added).

Elder George Q. Cannon spoke of the power associated with the presence and influence of temples:

> Every foundation stone that is laid for a Temple, and every Temple completed according to the order the Lord has revealed for His Holy Priesthood, lessens the power of Satan on the earth and increases the power of God and Godliness, moves the heavens in mighty power in our behalf, invokes and calls down upon us the blessings of the Eternal Gods and those who reside in Their presence (*Gospel Truth*, 2:111).

A Pentecostal Endowment

While the temple was being completed and dedicated in Kirtland, the heavens were opened in ways that enabled a great number of the Saints to experience many spiritual manifestations. This plethora of extraterrestrial activities was described by Joseph Smith, following a meeting he attended on March 30, 1836:

> I left the meeting in the charge of the Twelve, and retired about nine o'clock in the evening. The brethren continued exhorting, prophesying, and speaking in tongues until five o'clock in the morning. The Savior made His appearance to some, while angels ministered to others, and it was a Pentecost and an endowment indeed, long to be remembered, for the sound shall go forth from this place into all the world, and the occurrences of this day shall be handed down upon the pages of sacred history, to all generations; as the day of Pentecost, so shall this day be numbered and celebrated as a

year of jubilee, and time of rejoicing to the Saints of the Most High God (*HC,* 2:432–33).

Illustrative of some of the happenings that took place are these selected narratives:

Joseph Smith: "Many of my brethren who received the ordinance with me saw glorious visions also. Angels ministered unto them as well as to myself, and the power of the Highest rested upon us, the house [temple] was filled with the glory of God, and we shouted Hosanna to God and the Lamb. My scribe also received his anointing with us, and saw, in a vision, the armies of heaven protecting the Saints . . . and many things which I saw" (*HC,* 2:381).

Prescindia Huntington: "In Kirtland we enjoyed many very great blessings, and often saw the power of God manifested. On one occasion I saw angels clothed in white walking upon the temple. It was during one of our monthly fast meetings, when the saints were in the temple worshiping. A little girl came to my door and in wonder called me out, exclaiming, 'The meeting is on the top of the meeting house!' I went to the door, and there I saw on the temple angels clothed in white covering the roof from end to end. They seemed to be walking to and fro; they appeared and disappeared. The third time they appeared and disappeared before I realized that they were not mortal men. Each time in a moment they vanished, and their reappearance was the same. This was in broad daylight, in the afternoon. A number of the children in Kirtland saw the same. When the brethren and sisters came home in the evening, they told of the power of God manifested in the temple that day, and of the prophesying and speaking in tongues" (*The Women of Mormondom,* 207).

Joseph Smith: While in the Kirtland Temple on Jan. 21, 1836, Joseph had a vision of the celestial kingdom. He saw his deceased brother Alvin, his parents (who were then still alive), Adam and Abraham, God the Father, and His Son, Jesus Christ. The account of the vision was published in Joseph's history of the Church (see *HC,* 2:380) but has since been canonized as scripture and is presently published as Doctrine and Covenants 137.

Many Latter-day Saints have assumed that when the Lord said He would endow the Saints with power, He had reference only to the priesthood ordinance provided in temples, known as the endowment. Without question, that ordinance is included as part of the fulfillment of the Lord's promise. However, since the full endowment ordinance was not provided to the people in the Kirtland Temple, there must be a broader spectrum of the ways the Lord is able to endow His people with power from on high. President David O. McKay said, ". . . there is inherent *in the restored gospel* the greatest spiritualizing power ever revealed to man" (*Treasures of Life,* 115; emphasis added). In the chapters that follow, we will discover that in addition to the role of temples, *there are many gospel principles and practices* that assist us in our quest to obtain spiritual power.

CHAPTER 2
THE NEED FOR POWER

During my years of service as a General Authority, I was frequently assigned by the First Presidency to interview people who had previously received priesthood ordinances in the temple but had then lost their Church membership. Subsequently, after completing the repentance process, they had been rebaptized and had applied for a restoration of their temple blessings. I was authorized to perform that priesthood ordinance pending the outcome of our interview. In my discussion with them, I always asked this question: "*Why* did the transgression occur that caused your loss of Church membership?" I assured them I was not asking for a rehearsal of *what* had happened. That information had already been discussed and evaluated by ward, stake, and general Church priesthood leaders. My desire was to know what they considered to be the *reasons* for their sinful behavior.

Typically, their answers included an explanation of the circumstances they previously faced and failed to handle appropriately. Sometimes they linked their problem to financial stress, sometimes to moral temptation and opportunity, or perhaps they had yielded to feelings of loneliness or a perceived lack of appreciation and understanding on the part of a spouse. But these kinds of descriptions were simply restatements of the facts associated with *what* had happened. I needed to be sure they understood *why* they had yielded to the tempting invitations they had encountered before. After all, if they didn't know why they were weak enough to become involved, they would likely not fortify themselves and thus be protected against some future exposure to situations that might entice them to fall again.

By this time in our discussion, most of the individuals did not know what I was getting at and did not know how to respond to my question. So I said I would help them discover the key. I reminded them that at the time they faced their temptation, they surely must have recognized the possibility and sensed the likelihood of their participation in wrongdoing. Since they had previously been active Church members and had received priesthood ordinances in the temple, they had been clearly taught the enormity of the sins with which they were tampering and had certainly been counseled to avoid even the very appearance of evil. They knew what they were considering was wrong. Yet, when they knew they should not, why could they not resist? In each interview, I selected a few of the following questions for them to consider.

Before permitting yourself to yield to temptations you knew were wrong:

• Did you fast and pray for the Lord to help you avoid involvement in sorrow-producing behavior? Did you ask your spouse and family to join you in that request of the Lord?

• Did you gather your family around you in home evening settings and in family activities that you might gain strength from their association?

• Were you diligently searching your scriptures for divine direction to guide you through the traps of temptations?

• Did you go to the temple to feel the Spirit in that holy place and receive inspired insights from your all-wise Heavenly Father?

• Were you regularly attending your sacrament meetings to gain strength from the Holy Spirit through the renewal of your covenants?

• Did you counsel with your bishop about this hazardous condition?

• Did you listen to and review counsel and instruction from our living Apostles and prophets on these critical issues?

• Did you seek to avoid associating with the wrong kind of people or being exposed to destructive influences that could result in your downfall?

• Did you seek opportunity to lose yourself in the service of others, especially in being faithful in Church callings?

• Were you adhering to Word of Wisdom standards and paying a full tithe?

• Were you being honest in your dealings with others?

• Were you striving to be worthy of the Lord's help in your personal life?

• Were you humble in your heart and sincere in your desire to avoid sin?

All of those interviewed had to admit they had not been engaged in a lifestyle pleasing to the Lord. They then came to understand *why* they had fallen into sin. The reason was simple. They were not living so as to develop and possess sufficient spiritual power to recognize, resist, and overcome satanic influences. Forces of evil had gained power over them. In most cases, they had even lost the desire to avoid involvement in sin.

This process is sometimes a slow spiritual death, often begun and then perpetuated by one of Satan's most insidious and destructive tools—deception. When we first encounter temptations or circumstances that entice us to participate in evil and wrongful practices, we may not see them as being of serious consequence, and we thereby fail to realize the potential results. If we don't consider the situation to be serious we will likely allow ourselves to indulge in small sins, thinking nothing big will come of it. Rationalization or self-justification takes the place of clear thinking and evaluation. Commonly, the person justifies his or her wrongdoing long enough that he or she actually believes it to be all right. The truth is, the individual has been deceived into accepting wrongful doing as an acceptable practice. Such was the experience of both Sherem (see Jacob 7:18) and Korihor (see Alma 30:52–53). The Prophet Joseph Smith said, "The devil has no power over us only as we permit him. The moment we revolt at anything which comes from God, the devil takes power" (*TPJS*, 181).

From a beloved hymn, we remember this teaching: "There is peace in righteous doing. Choose the right! There's safety for the soul. Choose the right in all labors you're pursuing; Let God and heaven be your goal" (*Hymns*, no. 239). Whereas peace prevails in righteous doing, "There is no peace, saith the Lord, unto the wicked" (Isa. 48:22).

In reality there is a rejection of the Lord's teachings in exchange for Satan's suggestions, though we probably do not consciously identify which of these two authors is the source of the opposing ideas. Often, we are not willing to honestly scrutinize our thoughts and behavior to determine if they are right or wrong. Sometimes, however, we just continue what we are doing because we enjoy doing so, even though we know it is wrong. We reject the idea of changing course and consequently become more deeply involved. Small things become big things and, with continued participation, become a part of one's lifestyle. Elder Spencer W. Kimball taught the following:

> Whoever suggested that the little white sweet berry was tasteless or the mistletoe without color? How else would it attract? How else would it be propagated and spread? Whoever said that sin was not fun? Whoever claimed that Lucifer was not handsome, persuasive, easy, friendly? Whoever said that sin was unattractive, undesirable, or nauseating in its acceptance?
>
> Transgression wears elegant gowns and sparkling apparel. It is highly perfumed, has attractive features, a soft voice. It is found in educated circles and sophisticated groups. It provides sweet and comfortable luxuries. Sin is easy and has a big company of bed fellows. It promises immunity from restrictions, temporary freedoms. It can momentarily satisfy hunger, thirst, desire, urges, passions, wants, without immediately paying the price. But, it begins tiny and grows to monumental proportions. It grows drop by drop, inch by inch (CR, Apr. 1961, 66).

For us to avoid falling into sinful practices we must have a desire to recognize spiritual hazards and be capable of accurately identifying the source of persuasive influences. If we are seeking direction from the Lord and are living in such a way that we can recognize His guidance, we will not be deceived. One of the common themes the Lord provides in the scriptures is His frequent reference to revealed patterns and principles, that His people might understand truth and not be deceived (see D&C 1:24; 43:6; 45:57; 46:8; 50:15–23; 52:14–19; Moro. 7:12–28).

The Lord does not permit Satan to represent false ideas as truth without the Lord first teaching eternal truths and providing His people with means to detect any form of disguised evil or satanic counterfeits (see D&C 93:40, 42; Alma 12:32). Anyone who understands truth cannot be deceived into thinking wrong is right. Each person has agency to decide whether to live the Lord's way. But if that person falls into sin, it is because of his or her choosing to do so, not because he or she had been prevented from knowing the truth.

Each of us should remember that Satan's motives are to deceive and destroy, whereas the Savior provides detection of and deliverance from the evil one. Lucifer does not support those who choose to follow him (see Alma 30:60). Instead, he and his angels laugh and rejoice because of their conquering success with some of the Lord's children (see 3 Ne. 9:2). In contrast, the prophet Mormon taught the Lord's way:

> The Lord God prepareth the way that the residue of men may have faith in Christ, that the Holy Ghost may have place in their hearts, *according to the power thereof;* and after this manner bringeth to pass the Father, the covenants which he hath made unto the children of men.
>
> And Christ hath said: If ye will have faith in me *ye shall have power to do whatsoever thing is expedient in me* (Moro. 7:32–33; emphasis added).

During the discussions I mentioned earlier, I shared the Lord's warning concerning the future decreed status of non-repentant, unclean people: "And now, behold, I say unto you, never at any time have I declared from mine own mouth that they should return [unto me], for where I am they cannot come, *for they have no power*" (D&C 29:29; emphasis added).

It isn't only the Lord that denies them entry into His eternal kingdom. They have closed the gates on themselves by failing to reach needed levels of spirituality. They render themselves incapable of living in celestial environments (see Alma 12:14). They have failed to obtain the enabling spiritual power.

Gratefully, the good people I met with were able to realize the folly of their failure to fortify and protect themselves. During the course of our interview, the individuals reaffirmed their determination to adhere to the Lord's protective plan, thus becoming recipients of resulting spiritual power. Blessings were then restored to them with confidence that in the future they could have sufficient power to identify and resist evil influences and keep their sacred covenants intact.

All of us would be wise to apply insights provided by President Harold B. Lee in his last general conference address. "Where is there safety in the world today? . . . There is only one place of safety and that is within the *realm of the power of Almighty God* that he gives to those who keep his commandments and listen to his voice, as he speaks through the channels that he has ordained for that purpose" (CR, Oct. 1973, 169; emphasis added). The channels mentioned by President Lee consist of three primary means the Lord has established to convey His will to his people, the combined content of which constitutes the gospel of Jesus Christ (see D&C 52:9, 36; Jacob 4:6):

1. Scripture

2. Living prophets

3. The Holy Ghost

As President Lee declared, those who hearken to the Lord's voice through these channels have access to His power. It should be remembered that Paul taught that "the gospel of Christ . . . is the **power of God unto salvation** to every one that believeth" (Rom. 1:16; emphasis added).

Elder Bruce R. McConkie taught the following:

We are not saved by church programs as such, by church organizations alone, or even by the Church itself. It is the gospel that saves. . . . The gospel is the plan of salvation by which we can change the souls we possess into the kind of souls *who can go where God and Christ are.* Paul tells us that the gospel comes to men in two ways—in word and in power [see 1 Thess. 1:5]. The word of the gospel is written in the scriptures; *the power of the gospel* is written in the lives of those who both receive and enjoy the gift of the Holy Ghost ("Holy Writ: Published Anew," Regional Representative Seminar, Apr. 2, 1982, 1; emphasis added).

Elder McConkie further emphasized:

O how this truth needs to be thundered into the ears of every living soul. The kingdom of God on earth, the Church of Jesus Christ, the gospel of salvation, are not found in word but in power. It matters that a people have the word of God, that the Bible is open before them, that they have a record of what God and angels have said, that they know what the doctrines of salvation are. There is no salvation in these things standing alone. Of course men must have the word; of course they must learn the doctrines of salvation. *But men do not gain the kingdom of*

God, the Church, or the gospel until they possess the power.
The gospel is the power of God unto salvation. There must
be priesthood, the gift of the Holy Ghost, revelation,
visions, miracles, glorious manifestations of God's power, or
there is no kingdom of God, no Church of Jesus Christ, no
saving gospel. Where God's power is manifest, there is the
Church and kingdom of God on earth, and where his
power is not found, there the Church and kingdom is not
(*DNTC*, Vol. 2, 333; emphasis added).

Lucifer only has power over us when we permit him to plant
his plans and powers within us. If we surround ourselves with the
protecting mantle of gospel principles and practices and nourish
those seeds of truth and light, spiritual power from on high
provides a formidable barrier preventing penetration of our being
by foreign powers seeking destruction of our soul.

CHAPTER 3
GIVE ME THY POWER

In chapter two, we learned why there is an absolute need to have spiritual power. Now we need to know something of the way by which we can obtain it. In two separate scriptural passages, the Savior provides an insight for us that opens a magnificent view of the enabling process of accessing heavenly powers.

While speaking to Moses concerning an encounter with Lucifer in the premortal world, the Lord, speaking for the Father, said:

> [Satan] came before me, saying—Behold, here am I, send me, I will be thy son, and I will redeem all mankind, that one soul shall not be lost, and surely I will do it; wherefore give me thine *honor*. . . .
>
> Wherefore, because that Satan rebelled against me, and sought to destroy the agency of man, which I, the Lord God, had given him, and also, that I should give unto him mine own *power;* by the power of mine Only Begotten, I caused that he should be cast down (Moses 4:1, 3; emphasis added).

In a revelation given to Joseph Smith, the Lord referred again to the time of premortal existence, and spoke of the devil saying that while living there, "he [the devil] rebelled against me, saying,

Give me thine *honor,* which is my *power*" (D&C 29:36; emphasis added).

In both accounts, the Lord equated His and His Father's honor with Their power. In considering how the word "honor" might be applied to the Lord, one might think of the high regard or esteem in which He is held by all who know of Him and His role in the Father's eternal plan of happiness and salvation. Certainly we honor Him for all He is and all He has done. But that perspective would fall short of having a viable equation with His power.

Another way of thinking may provide more understanding of the connection between these two words. A person of honor is one who has integrity, is true to his commitments, and valiant in his responsibilities. An honorable person is one who is loyal and worthy of being trusted. A scriptural term reflecting these noble qualities of character is recorded in Matt. 1:19 referring to Mary's husband, Joseph. In this instance, the Greek word "dikaois" is translated as a "just man" or a "righteous being." This concept also appears in the Lord's description of exalted celestial beings when he said they are "just and true" (D&C 76:53). Joseph Smith declared that Latter-day Saints "believe in being honest [and] true" (Articles of Faith 1:13).

It is accurate to say that Jesus encompasses all these traits in His nature and has never failed to live by them. His every act has been and is an application of and obedience to His Father and to eternal laws and principles. He has never failed to be true to His covenants and loyal to His Father. He was described by the brother of Jared as "a God of truth, [who] canst not lie" (Ether 3:12). Jesus referred to his Father's role in the oath and covenant of the priesthood and said that He "cannot break" it (see D&C 84:40). To emphasize the eternal and never-changing nature of God's laws as well as God's own adherence to them, Alma declared that the works of justice could not be destroyed, and mercy could not rob justice or "God would cease to be God." He then reaffirmed that God does not cease to be God, thus providing us a basis for placing our trust, faith, and confidence in Him (see Alma 42:13, 22–23, 25). The Lord also taught this concept when He said, "The works, and the designs, and the purposes of God cannot be frustrated, neither can they come to naught.

"For God doth not walk in crooked paths, neither doth he turn to the right hand nor to the left, neither doth he vary from that which he hath said, therefore his paths are straight, and his course is one eternal round" (D&C 3:1–2).

Jesus has ordered His life to be one of honoring His Father's will, reflecting His Father's nature in His own, and faithfully fulfilling every facet of Father's plan. He has never strayed from the pathway defined by truth. Such commitment to honor has been the doorway by which His omnipotence has been attained. His life was one of strict obedience rendered because He chose to do so. Some people obey when they are required to, but would not if they could choose. This obedience is doing the right thing for the wrong reason. Though such obedient behavior is better than being disobedient for any reason, Elder Richard G. Scott warns of the consequence attached to such choices. He declares, "Forced obedience yields no enduring fruit" (BYU Education Week, Aug. 21, 2007).

When we consider what Lucifer was requesting, it is apparent what he was doing. When he asked to be given Jesus' honor, what he really sought was the power that accompanied that honor. He did not want to pay the price of obedience Jesus paid to attain it, but did want the fruits of the labor without being a laborer. He sought for power, but would not subscribe to the prerequisite process of bending his will and molding his nature to be a reflection of the

Father. When his proposal to have power over Father's children was rejected, he was furious and rebelled against God's Firstborn Son (see D&C 76:25).

Jesus had the authority of His Father to do all things in His behalf. So when Lucifer rebelled against Jesus, he was rebelling against presiding priesthood authority. Consequently, Lucifer was cast out of heaven—not for transgressing, but for rebelling. Transgressors can be forgiven when they repent. But rebels alienate themselves from presiding authority and refuse to yield to directives or counsel from that authority and will not change. The issue is not that they can't repent when they do wrong; the problem is that they won't. That's what rebellion is. It is a dangerous practice to be rebellious. Even so-called small, deliberate departures from heeding counsel of priesthood authority can cause a corresponding loss of spirituality and establish a pattern of justifying contrary behavior.

When a prophet counsels on any subject, it is well for us to check our response. If we are not compliant, we should determine the reason why our behavior is out of harmony with presiding priesthood authority. Sometimes we might hear ourselves make statements of rationalization like, "It is just his opinion," or "That issue doesn't really matter," or "Everybody is doing it." Let us remember that if we fail to follow divine directives through priesthood channels of authority, we are falling into the category of rebellion. From time to time, most of us sing the words of a hymn, "We thank thee, O God, for a prophet, to guide us in these latter days" (*Hymns,* no. 19). Since the song of the righteous is a prayer unto the Lord (see D&C 25:12), we should be careful that we are not being hypocritical by rebelling against prophetic guidance.

Lucifer's request of the Lord to give him His honor or power is like unto the five foolish virgins who said to the five wise virgins, "Give us of your oil" (Matt. 25:8). President Spencer W. Kimball said the oil represents spiritual preparedness that comes from right-eous living and therefore cannot be shared or given by one person to another. He asked,

> How can one share obedience to the principle of tithing; a mind at peace from righteous living; an accumulation of knowledge? How can one share faith or testimony? How can one share attitudes or chastity, or the experience of a mission? How can one share temple privileges? . . . In our lives the oil of preparedness is accumulated drop by drop in righteous living. Attendance at sacrament meetings adds oil to our lamps, drop by drop over the years. Fasting, family prayer, home teaching, control of bodily appetites, preaching the gospel, studying the scriptures—each act of dedication and obedience is a drop added to our store. Deeds of kind-ness, payment of offerings and tithes, chaste thoughts and actions, marriage in the covenant for eternity—these, too, contribute importantly to the oil with which we can at midnight refuel our exhausted lamps (*Faith Precedes the Miracle*, 255–56).

The Lord could not share His honor any more than we can expect others to provide us with spiritual strength. We either attain it through our faithful adherence to eternal principles and covenants, or we remain barren of that precious power. President Brigham Young strongly emphasized this need when he said,

> Now those men, or those women, who know no more about the power of God, and the influence of the Holy Spirit, than to be led entirely by another person, suspending their own understanding, and pinning their fate upon

another's sleeve, will never be capable of entering into the celestial glory, to be crowned as they anticipate, they will never be capable of becoming Gods. They cannot rule themselves to say nothing of ruling others, but they must be dictated to in every trifle, like a child. They cannot control themselves in the least, but James, Peter, or somebody else must control them. They never can hold scepters of glory, majesty, and power in the celestial kingdom. Who will? Those who are valiant and inspired with the true independence of heaven, who will go forth boldly in the service of their God, leaving others to do as they please, determined to do right, though all mankind besides should take the opposite course (*JD,* 11:312).

Though the Lord cannot bestow His honor upon us, He has provided us the means by which we can obtain our own. It is an attainable condition that each of us might develop while in this state of mortality. How comforting and exhilarating are the feelings that come into the soul of one determined to possess the power of righteous independence. President Ezra Taft Benson provided both perspective and promise as he declared: "When obedience ceases to be an irritant and becomes our quest, in that moment God will endow us with power" (quoted by Elder Donald L. Staheli in CR, Apr. 1998, 108).

CHAPTER 4
THE POWER OF A TESTIMONY OF CHRIST

One of the most insightful presentations of mankind's mortal experience is recorded in the Book of Mormon. It is portrayed as symbolic imagery in the prophet Lehi's dream or vision (see 1 Ne. 8:2–36). Contained within that presentation is a marvelous manifestation of the need for the power about which we have been speaking as well as a specific identification of the source of that power.

Lehi identified four groups of people in his dream. First were those who began to follow a path leading toward a tree but never did arrive. When mists of darkness overshadowed them, they wandered off the path and were lost. A second group took hold of an iron rod that ran along the path leading to the tree and thus were able to safely get through the mists of darkness that obscured the path and still remain on course. After arriving at the tree, they partook of the fruit growing thereon. But when they became objects of scorn and ridicule from other people, they felt ashamed, fell away into forbidden paths, and were lost.

A third group traveled the same path, held onto the same iron rod and partook of the fruit of the same tree, but *they* heeded not the scorn and scoffing and so remained steadfast. The fourth group made no effort to get to the tree at all. Instead, they sought out a

large and spacious building from which they pointed fingers of
scorn at those who were partakers of the fruit of the tree.

Note that all elements of the environment in the dream are the
same for everyone. The only variable is the attitude or reaction of the
people concerning the tree. The significance of that fact is emphasized in a conversation between Lehi's son Nephi and a heavenly
messenger, as recorded in 1 Nephi, chapter 11. The messenger asked
Nephi, "What desirest thou?" (verse 2). He responded in verse three
by saying he desired to behold the things his father had seen. And
then came the critical question. "And the Spirit said unto me:
Believest thou that thy father saw the tree of which he hath spoken?"
(verse 4). Of all the symbolic imagery in that dream, the heavenly
spirit asked only about the tree. He did not ask about the rod, the
path, the mists of darkness, or the spacious building. He asked about
Nephi's belief concerning the tree. The selection of the object in the
question provides a message of priority. After all, the tree is the
center of focus about which everything else in the dream revolves.

Nephi then responded to the question by saying he did believe
there was a tree, even though he hadn't seen it. The Spirit's
response to Nephi's answer is most interesting. The Spirit declared,
"Blessed art thou Nephi, *because thou believest in the Son of the most
high God . . .*" (verse 6; emphasis added). Nephi learned that his
declaration of belief in the existence of the tree was equivalent to a
statement of belief in the Son of God.

The Spirit continued to reinforce the meaning of the symbolic
tree by telling Nephi that after he should *behold the tree* he would
see a man descending out of heaven of whom he should bear
record that *"it is the Son of God"* (verse 7; emphasis added). The
tree is a sign or symbol of the Savior.

The heavenly messenger shows Nephi a number of other
things, including a view of the virgin mother of the Son of God.

Then he sees her with her baby, and an angel declares, "Behold the Lamb of God, yea, even *the Son of the Eternal Father*! Knowest thou *the meaning of the tree*?" (verse 21; emphasis added). In other words, the angel is asking, "Nephi, after three illustrations, do you now know the meaning of the tree?" The tree really is a symbolic representation of Jesus Christ, the Son of God.

In the next verse, Nephi declared that the tree represented the love of God. It is a most meaningful answer, because the love of God has never been more greatly manifested than in the life and mission of the Savior and His Atonement. The symbolic connection between the tree and the Savior is reinforced when the prophet Alma recorded the Savior's invitation: "Come unto me and ye shall partake of the fruit of the tree of life" (Alma 5:34).

A major message of that dream is that the behavior of people revolves around their perspective of and relationship with Christ. The role of Christ and His Atonement in one's mortal life is the focus of the entire dream. The four groups of people could also be further classified into two groups:

1. Those who come to the Savior and remain true and faithful to that which they receive from Him.

2. Those who either do not come or do not remain true to Him.

These two categories would account for all people who live or who have lived in the mortal world.

President David O. McKay taught in a general conference address: "What you sincerely in your heart think of Christ will determine what you are, will largely determine what your acts will be" (CR, Apr. 1951, 93). This concept reflects the level of our faith in Christ as well as our knowledge and conviction of His role in the Father's plan of salvation, for they are all determinants of our nature and behavior. Those same considerations provide the basis for the acquisition and development of our spiritual power. For instance, Nephi recorded that his father, Lehi, spoke with spiritual power, then noted that he received that power "by faith on the Son of God" (1 Ne. 10:17). Now what about the iron rod? When his brothers asked what it symbolized, Nephi said, "It was the word of God; and whoso would hearken unto the word of God, and would hold fast unto it, they would never perish; neither could the temptations and the fiery darts of the adversary overpower them unto blindness, to lead them away to destruction" (1 Ne. 15:24).

Over the years, it has been my privilege to conduct interviews with Church members seeking temple recommends. Some interesting patterns developed. I always asked, "Are you a full tithe payer?" Some have said, "Oh, that is an easy one. There are some requirements of the gospel that are hard, but tithing is easy for me." Yet other people struggle to pay tithing. I always asked, "Do you keep the Word of Wisdom?" Some would say, "Oh, that is no problem, never has been." Still others have had a hard time keeping the Word of Wisdom. Those who have faith in the word of God and hold onto its provisions and promises have the power to be faithful to the Lord's teachings; but those lacking faith in the Lord and His laws are overpowered by the powers of darkness and fail to make or keep covenants with God.

Like the various symbolic elements in Lehi's dream, gospel laws are the same for everyone: tithing, Word of Wisdom, chastity, or any other principle of the gospel. For some people, those laws are stepping stones to spiritual growth and power, while others find those same requirements to be stumbling blocks that create difficult obstacles in their lives.

What makes the difference? The dream of Lehi teaches the lesson, and President McKay answers the question. What one thinks of Christ is the key factor. It is the greatest single influence that determines what we are and do, whether it be good or bad, right or wrong. This concept is a major theme that recurs frequently in the scriptures. In the balance of this chapter, we will look at some selected passages as illustrations.

In the very first verse of the Book of Mormon, Nephi spoke of his parents and referred to them as "goodly parents" (1 Ne. 1:1). In the same family were two brothers by the names of Laman and Lemuel. How did they describe their parents? "They did murmur in many things against their father, because he was a visionary man," saying that he did things "because of the foolish imaginations of his heart" (1 Ne. 2:11). Same father; same family. What made the difference in how Nephi saw his father and how Laman and Lemuel looked at him? We read, "And thus Laman and Lemuel, being the eldest, did murmur against their father . . . *because they knew not the dealings of that God who had created them*" (1 Ne. 2:12; emphasis added). What they thought of Christ determined their attitude toward their father. In their case, it was the absence of a knowledge of God and His works. That is what made the difference in the kind of persons they were and how they perceived others.

Nephi was asked to return to Jerusalem and obtain the plates of brass from Laban. His response was, "I will go and do the things which the Lord hath commanded" (1 Ne. 3:7). Who did Nephi say commanded him? The Lord. Who actually spoke to Nephi and asked him to go back to get the records? His own father. Nephi did not say he would go and do the things his father asked of him. He said he would do as the Lord commanded (through Lehi, His representative and spokesman). As a comparison, who did Laman and Lemuel think wanted them to go? Lehi told Nephi, "Behold thy brothers murmur, saying it is a hard thing which I have required of them; but behold I have not required it of them, but it is a commandment of the Lord" (1 Ne. 3:5). It mattered who Nephi thought commanded him. So what did Nephi think of Christ when he knew the assignment came from Him? He knew the Lord would not give a commandment they could not fulfill, and He would prepare a way for them to do so. Consequently, he refused to give up until they had accomplished the Lord's request.

Undoubtedly, Nephi gave the assignment his best effort. But maybe Laman and Lemuel did also. And perhaps Nephi was not stronger, wiser, or more clever than his brothers. But the success of the mission did not solely depend on the young men doing their best. They also needed the Lord to help them go beyond what they could offer as skills and abilities by providing His help and power where needed.

President Spencer W. Kimball provided some great insights in connection with this incident with the brass plates:

> Remember how Nephi was confronted with an impossible situation and could not get the plates. His brothers could not. They were unable to buy them. They could not bribe them out of the hands of Laban. They could not force their way in, and their lives were hanging on a thread. In spite of all of that, here comes one unarmed boy who walks into a city through a wall that could not be penetrated, into the gates that could not be opened, into a garden that was impenetrable, into a vault that was locked among soldiers who could not be bypassed, and he came out with his arms full of records to keep his posterity and others from perishing in unbelief. He did what was humanly impossible.

But nothing is impossible to the Lord. Anytime we have him on our side, when he has called us and given us a commandment, then, if our energy and our efforts and our planning and our prayers are equal to the size of the calling, the work, of course, will be successfully completed (*Relief Society Magazine,* Apr. 1959, 217–18).

We should ask ourselves this question: "Who called us individually in our present Church duties and assignments, the bishop or the stake president or the Lord?" Does it make any difference how we answer the question? What one thinks of Christ determines whether we have access to sufficient power (as Nephi did) and are committed enough (as Nephi was) to make our callings stepping stones to successful completion of duties and assignments or stumbling blocks with resultant failure.

Nephi was asked to keep a second set of records (see 1 Ne. 9:3–5). What reason did the Lord give Nephi for keeping that second set? Nephi stated he did not know the purpose. Why then would Nephi do what was a very difficult task without understanding a reason? His motivation could not just be that he was commanded. There are many people who are commanded to do things but do not do them. Nephi did what he was commanded because of what he thought of Jesus Christ. Notice what he thought of Him: "The Lord knoweth all things from the beginning; wherefore, he prepareth a way to accomplish all his works. He hath all power unto the fulfilling of all his words" (1 Ne. 9:6). Subsequently, Nephi recorded that "[the Savior] knoweth all things, and there is not anything save he knows it" (2 Ne. 9:20).

One of the more common doctrinal issues that is often misunderstood is whether the Lord knows all things. Some people have conceded that He knows all things about some things, but may not know all things about all things. Nephi thought that He knows all things about all things. Does it matter if the Lord knows all things? Further, does it matter if we know whether He does? The Prophet Joseph Smith taught, "Without the knowledge of all things, God would not be able to save any portion of his creatures, and were it not for the idea existing in the minds of men that God has all knowledge, it would be impossible for them to exercise faith in Him unto salvation" (*Lectures on Faith,* 4th lecture, paragraph 11). Unless we think of Christ and His attributes with true understanding, we cannot develop and exercise faith in Him. And unless we have faith in Him, we cannot develop or access spiritual power.

Because of what Nephi thought of Christ, he had the faith to prepare a second set of records providing knowledge of the early spiritual Nephite history, thus becoming a stepping stone for all of the generations in this dispensation twenty-four centuries later. Otherwise, the loss of 116 pages of Book of Mormon manuscript by Martin Harris would have been a stumbling block by preventing our access to information recorded only in the first set of Nephite records (see headings to D&C 3 and 10; see also D&C 10:38–45).

Nephi wrote about the plain and precious things that were taken out of the Bible. Missing from the current biblical text are prophecies, covenants, and testimonies of Jesus Christ as the Messiah, Redeemer, and Savior of the world (see 1 Ne. 13:23–26; see also Editorial Page, *Church News,* Jan. 22, 1966). These precious things were removed by those who did not love the Savior or believe in His teachings. Their negative feelings toward Christ determined what they did. Nephi described the result of their actions: "Because of these things which are taken away out of the gospel of the Lamb, an exceedingly great many do stumble, yea, insomuch that Satan hath great power over them" (1 Ne. 13:29). What one person thought of Christ became a stumbling block for many others. Satan's power over them was made possible by the lack of their spiritual power.

Listen to two different accounts of the journeys of Lehi's family through the wilderness. One is a description of the experience through the eyes of Laman and Lemuel, and the other is Nephi's report of the same experience:

Laman and Lemuel — These two brothers said to Nephi:

And thou art like unto our father, led away by the foolish imaginations of his heart; yea, he hath led us out of the land of Jerusalem, and we have wandered in the wilderness for these many years; and our women have toiled, being big with child; and they have borne children in the wilderness and suffered all things, save it were death; and it would have been better that they had died before they came out of Jerusalem than to have suffered these afflictions.

Behold, these many years we have suffered in the wilderness, which time we might have enjoyed our possessions and the land of our inheritance; yea, and we might have been happy (1 Ne. 17:20–21).

Nephi —

We did again take our journey in the wilderness. . . . And we did travel and wade through much affliction in the wilderness; and our women did bear children in the wilderness.

And so great were the blessings of the Lord upon us, that while we did live upon raw meat in the wilderness, our women did give plenty of suck for their children, and were strong, yea, even like unto the men; and they began to bear their journeyings without murmurings. . . .

If it so be that the children of men keep the commandments of God he doth nourish them, and strengthen them, and provide means whereby they can accomplish the thing which he has commanded them; wherefore, he did provide means for us while we did sojourn in the wilderness (1 Ne. 17:1–3).

It doesn't sound like these people were on the same trip. Isn't it interesting that Laman, Lemuel, and Nephi went on the same journey, walked the same trails, partook of the same food, experienced the same climate and temperatures, and slept on the same ground. Yet some of them complained of suffering afflictions, while others said they waded through afflictions and the Lord blessed them. What made the difference? It was what they thought of Christ that determined if they had sufficient spiritual power from on high. Laman and Lemuel said their father led them, whereas Nephi was led by the Lord.

People react differently to afflictions. For instance, we read, "Behold, because of the exceedingly great length of the war between the Nephites and the Lamanites many had become hardened . . . and many were softened because of their afflictions" (Alma 62:41). The war was the same length for all people; yet out of the same experience, many were hardened and many were softened. For some, the war was a stepping stone, and for others, it became a stumbling block. What makes the difference? By now, we know the answer.

Listen to Alma bear his testimony: "I do know that whosoever shall put their trust in God shall be supported in their trials, and their troubles, and their afflictions, and shall be lifted up at the last day" (Alma 36:3). If we do not have faith in the Savior, it is hard for us to trust Him. The usual trust test comes when what He asks us to do is difficult or is something we don't want to do, or when we don't understand the need. Then our judgment often determines our behavior. It is difficult to trust Him and His promises if we are not convinced of His nature and power to fulfill. I wonder how many of us would go to the temple if our decision to go depended on tangible evidence that what we do there has any bearing on anyone's life after death, ours or the dead. It is a trust level based on faith in the Savior, which in turn is based on what we think of Him.

For those who trust the Lord, there is a promise of support in our afflictions. Certainly the promise is not one of immunity from trials for faithful Saints. Most of us suffer afflictions like everyone else. The Lord may or may not remove unwanted or untimely burdens from our lives. He may or may not lighten our load. But one thing *is* certain: He will provide the power that increases our capacity to carry burdens (see Mosiah 24:14–15; Alma 33:23).

Here is another example of the principle discussed in this chapter. Many people in the world do not believe Jesus speaks through prophets today. Generally, their attitude is that His voice was silenced some time in the distant past, and He is no longer being heard. Such a philosophy creates a barrier preventing them from obtaining the very spiritual power they could and need to possess. For instance, the Savior has testified that the Book of Mormon is true (see D&C 17:6). He has said that Joseph Smith was and is His prophet (see D&C 1:17; 136:37–39), and that The Church of Jesus Christ of Latter-day Saints is "the only true and living church upon the face of the whole earth" (D&C 1:30). Consider the power of the Spirit that is available to those who think the Savior is a living Christ who spoke those words and who continues to speak to His prophets. Yet, anyone thinking otherwise will find that the Book of Mormon, the Prophet Joseph Smith, the LDS Church, and the Savior Himself are stumbling blocks. How sad indeed.

In the latter years of the reign of King Benjamin, the rising generation was described as people who *would not* be baptized, and *would not* join the church, and *would not* pray (see Mosiah 26:4). "Would nots" are usually rebellious people. But wisdom dictates the need to look beyond the performance level and ask *why* they would not. Interestingly, the preceding verses provide valuable insights to the problem. First of all, we read that they "*did not believe* . . . concerning the resurrection of the dead, *neither did they believe* concerning the coming of Christ. And now because of their unbelief [lack of faith] they *could not understand* the word of God; and their hearts were hardened" (Mosiah 26:2–3; emphasis added). So their rebellion and unwillingness to live in accordance with gospel teachings was because they could not understand those teachings; and the reason they could not understand the word of God was that they did not believe or have faith in Christ.

Again we see that what a person sincerely thinks of Christ determines what he/she really is and what he/she will do. Failing to adhere to gospel principles is a stumbling block caused by a lack of spiritual power in the life of the individual which, in turn, is a result of a faulty perspective of Christ. Whenever we attempt to help such people as described above, we want to avoid treating behavioral symptoms, and instead seek to correct the real cause—a lack of faith in Jesus Christ.

Since faith is always manifested by works, the absence of works reflects an absence of faith. Our efforts, then, need to be focused on the development and strengthening of faith in the Savior. The sons of Mosiah wanted to be a part of a mission to the Lamanites.

We read, "They were desirous that salvation should be declared to every creature, for they could not bear that any human soul should perish; yea, even the very thoughts that any soul should endure endless torment did cause them to quake and tremble" (Mosiah 28:3).

What determined their feelings and behavior? How did they come to understand the value of a soul that this verse describes? Their thoughts and feelings were created by their understanding of the Savior, His Atonement, and His mercy. This they learned by their own experience. What they thought of Christ became a stepping stone for thousands of Lamanites who were ultimately converted to the Lord through the missionary service of these sons of Mosiah. Yet these same young men, when they previously thought differently of the Lord, were a stumbling block to many Nephites and would have been to those same thousands of Lamanites. Instead, "as many as believed, or as many as were brought to the knowledge of the truth, through the preaching of Ammon and his brethren, according to the spirit of revelation and of prophecy, and *the power of God* working miracles in them—yea . . . as many of the Lamanites as believed in their preaching, and were converted unto the Lord, never did fall away" (Alma 23:6; emphasis added).

In this chapter, we have barely opened the door to a principle that is prevalent and frequently taught throughout the scriptures and through the teachings of our living prophets. Each of us can greatly benefit by diligently focusing on Jesus as the central figure of our lives. As we cling to the word of God and exercise faith in it, we shall have the spiritual power of obedience. We shall not stray, though mists of darkness may obscure our path. Though we may not see the object of our faith or our ultimate objective, our faith in Christ provides the power to attain all that has been promised to the faithful. May we thoughtfully and carefully respond to the question posed by the Savior to the pharisees: "What think ye of Christ?" (Matt. 22:42). The answer to that question is critical in developing our nature, our faith, and the power of righteous behavior while shaping our ultimate destiny.

CHAPTER 5
The Power of Knowledge About Christ

Often when I think of the Savior, I am reminded of an experience that took place while we were living and serving in Europe. On one occasion, my wife and I were traveling on a train in Germany and were sharing a compartment with a gentleman from Bulgaria. He spoke English, and we had a most pleasant visit as we passed the time together. We learned he was a professor of biochemistry at a university in Sofia, had been participating in a professional conference in Germany, and was then en route to his Bulgarian home. We told him of our ministerial assignments for the Church and shared with him some of our personal experiences in his country in connection with the development and influence of our church there.

Knowing of some of the religious restrictions imposed by Communist leaders for some forty years in his country, I took the opportunity to ask him if he personally had a belief in God. He quickly responded in the affirmative and said that he prayed with regularity. I asked a further question, "Do you also believe in Christ?" His answer astounded me. He confessed he did not know much about Him and then said, "But I don't suppose it matters if we know the details about Christ." I said to him, "Well, maybe the reason you feel that way is that you don't know the details about Christ." He agreed that would be a fair conclusion. I then suggested that he probably insisted that his students obtain a knowledge of the details about biochemistry before they could possibly hope to benefit by the knowledge that is available on that subject. He smiled and said, "I agree with you. I just hadn't considered it before."

We then spent a considerable amount of time discussing some of the details about Christ before we both changed trains and went our separate ways. After arriving back at my office in Frankfurt, I contacted the mission president in Bulgaria and arranged to have missionaries make contact with him and share more of what we know concerning the Savior and Redeemer of the world.

In my humble judgment, there is no subject known to man about which the details are more important to be known than those surrounding and associated with Jesus Christ. On the other hand, those of us who know of the powers of opposition should also expect to hear more misinformation and observe greater efforts to undermine and distort factual truths concerning Him than any other person in the earth's history. Because of the great visibility of His presiding position in the heavens, we should not be surprised when He is the primary target of satanic misrepresentation and false accusation. Many seek to reduce the Savior's image and discredit authentically recorded ministerial miracles by claiming them to be exaggerations, imaginations, or maybe allowing them to be just a little above the performance level of other well-known figures of human history. Even those who subscribe to the reality of the mortal existence of Jesus attempt to humanize Him rather than acknowledge Him as a God among men.

Let me share a few examples of this problem. First, from the writings of President Spencer W. Kimball: "The pastor of a church in Illinois said that he felt the same reverence for Santa Claus as he did for Jesus Christ and that he considered them both to be folk tales. . . . A noted professor emeritus in one of our largest universities said that 'Lazarus was not dead, but was merely "brought back to health" by Jesus, [through] the power of mind and learning, and by the "therapy of his own abundant vitality"'" (*Faith Precedes the Miracle,* 69).

On one occasion I walked by a classroom and noticed a Christian minister at the front of the room writing on the board the following statement: "Jesus was a **man** who claimed to be a God." I also remember standing on a street corner and being handed a newspaper by a member of a demonstrating religious group of young people. The front-page headline said this: "Jesus, the **Man** with the Plan." Probably many people are familiar with a book written by Bruce Barton who determined he would provide a portrayal of the life of Jesus better than he felt was being done in the Christian churches. But the title of the book is discouraging: "The **Man** Nobody Knows." Many depict Jesus as a man among men. And of course such an image would carry with it all of the limitations, weaknesses, and follies that beset all men everywhere. Bringing Jesus down to the level of a man is to divest Him of His divine nature with all of His attendant attributes and powers.

At a lecture given in Salt Lake City, a speaker questioned some of the recorded miracles of Jesus and suggested maybe biblical translations of the original manuscripts had exaggerated or twisted the truth. He said, "When Jesus walked on the water, for instance, did the original Aramaic say he 'waded' perhaps? And when he multiplied the loaves and fishes, did people in the crowd simply pull loaves of bread from beneath their robes?" (*Deseret News,* Nov. 25, 2000, Section E1).

It is little wonder that President Harold B. Lee chose to speak out on this subject. He noted conditions that existed in the earlier years of his life:

At that time there were the unmistakable evidences that there was coming into the religious world actually a question about the Bible and about the divine calling of the Master, Himself. Now fifty years later, *our greatest responsibility and anxiety is to defend the divine mission of our Lord and Master, Jesus Christ,* for all about us even among those who claim to be professors of the Christian faith, are [those who are] not willing to stand squarely in defense of the great truth that our Lord and Master, Jesus Christ, was indeed the Son of God (L.D.S.S.A. Fireside, Utah State University Campus, Oct. 10, 1971; emphasis added).

We cannot hope to defend the Savior's divine mission unless we know specific and meaningful details about Him and His mission. That we might be sufficiently and accurately informed, we refer to an angel's message delivered to King Benjamin about 125 years before the Savior's birth and note the many details he shared about Christ:

For behold, the time cometh, and is not far distant, that *with power,* the Lord Omnipotent who reigneth, who was, and is from all eternity to all eternity, shall come down from heaven among the children of men, and shall dwell in a tabernacle of clay, and shall go forth amongst men, working mighty miracles, such as healing the sick, raising the dead, causing the lame to walk, the blind to receive their sight, and the deaf to hear, and curing all manner of diseases.

And he shall cast out devils, or the evil spirits which dwell in the hearts of the children of men.

And lo, he shall suffer temptations, and pain of body,

hunger, thirst, and fatigue, *even more than man can suffer,* except it be unto death; for behold, blood cometh from every pore, so great shall be his anguish for the wickedness and the abominations of his people.

And he shall be called Jesus Christ, the Son of God, the Father of heaven and earth, the Creator of all things from the beginning; and his mother shall be called Mary.

And lo, he cometh unto his own, that salvation might come unto the children of men even through faith on his name; and even *after all this they shall consider him a man,* and say that he hath a devil, and shall scourge him, and shall crucify him.

And he shall rise the third day from the dead; and behold, he standeth to judge the world; and behold, all these things are done that a righteous judgment might come upon the children of men.

For behold, and also his blood atoneth for the sins of those who have fallen by the transgression of Adam, who have died not knowing the will of God concerning them, or who have ignorantly sinned.

But wo, wo unto him who knoweth that he rebelleth against God! For salvation cometh to none such except it be through repentance and faith on the Lord Jesus Christ (Mosiah 3:5–12; emphasis added).

From this extracted portion of one scripturally recorded sermon, we note some of the significant details about Christ:

1. He has **all power.**

2. He reigns over the heavens and earth.

3. His existence is forever.

4. He lived on this earth in a mortal body.

5. He worked mighty miracles **beyond the capacity of man.**

6. He suffered temptations and afflictions **beyond the capacity of man.**

7. He was the Son of God in the flesh; therefore He had the **power** to live and resurrect.

8. He was the son of a mortal woman; therefore He had the power to die.

9. His anguish for the world's sins caused blood to come from every pore.

10. He suffered an excruciating death.

11. He rose from the dead a resurrected personage.

12. He is the judge of the world.

13. His blood atoned for the sins of all mankind.

14. Salvation of all mankind depends upon their repentance and faith in Him.

And so we ask, does it matter that we know details about Christ? For instance, **if He did not have the *power* of a God, we could not obtain sufficient *power* from or through Him to attain unto our salvation. And if we did not know He had the *power*, we would not go to Him to obtain it.**

While serving as a mission president in the southern United States, I read an account of an interview between a major newspaper editor and the governor of one of the southern states where I served. The editor asked the questions, and the governor provided the answers. Following is a portion of an interview that took place shortly before one of the Easter seasons while I was there:

Editor: Are you a Christian?

Governor: Yes.

Editor: Do you believe Jesus died on the cross, was buried and resurrected?

Governor: No. I think Jesus died, but I don't believe he came back to life, because that's too much against natural law. I'm not going around preaching this, but he may have swooned, passed out or almost died, and when he was taken down, with superhuman strength, after a period of time he may have revived himself and come back to life. That has happened before. People appear to be dead, and then after a period of time will revive themselves. But I cannot embrace the idea that a person literally, actually died and then came back to life (*State Times,* Baton Rouge, Louisiana, Mar. 18, 1984).

We can compare the governor's statement denying the resurrection of Christ with the revealed details provided us by the Prophet Joseph Smith. Joseph and Sidney Rigdon were meditating together concerning the subject of the Resurrection, when a series of visions were opened to their view, the first of which was a vision of and an experience with the Savior. Following that experience, Joseph declared, "And now, after the many testimonies which have been given of him, this is the testimony, last of all, which we give of him: That he lives!" (D&C, 76:22).

Either the governor or Joseph Smith is wrong, but they cannot both be right. The governor expressed his opinion that it was not possible for Jesus to return to life with a physical, tangible, resurrected body. He would say no man has that power. And of course, if Jesus was not resurrected, then resurrection's door would remain forever closed to all the rest of Father's children. But Joseph's statement was not an expression of his opinion at all. It was a witness and testimony (created through personal experience) of a living, resurrected Christ based on four separate but congruent support pillars:

1. Listen to the words of the revelation recorded in Section 76: "For we saw him, even on the right hand of God" (verse 23). That statement was made eighteen centuries after the death of Jesus. There are many accounts of individuals who have received a testimony of the living reality of Christ based on having seen Him. It is an impressive and never-to-be-forgotten moment when someone says, "I have seen the Savior." I vividly recall hearing one of the Twelve, now deceased, make the following statement: "My testimony is the same as that of the apostle George Q. Cannon who said, 'I know that Jesus lives; for I have seen Him'" (*Gospel Truth*, 1:134).

2. The governor would probably respond to Joseph's witness by saying that he didn't doubt they saw someone, but how could they know it was Jesus? Joseph might answer such a question by reminding us that he had seen Jesus before in the sacred grove. But the words of the revelation make it clear: "We heard the voice bearing record that he is the Only Begotten of the Father" (verse 23). There was no chance of mistaken identity. They were told who it was they saw.

3. Perhaps the governor might challenge the experience as a hallucination and discount its validity. Once again, listen to the words of the revelation. Speaking of Jesus,

Joseph recorded: "Of whom we bear record; and the record which we bear is the fulness of the gospel of Jesus Christ, who is the Son, whom we saw and *with whom we conversed* in the heavenly vision" (verse 14; emphasis added). Jesus was there, all right—they talked with Him.

4. These first three pillars are impressive and impeccable. But the fourth is an even stronger foundation for the development of individual faith whether or not a person has an experience with seeing the Savior. Joseph said, "Now this caused us to marvel, for it was given unto us of the Spirit" (verse 18). The witnessing power of the Spirit is greater than sight or sound and is available to all honest seekers. All of us who have been recipients of the convincing power of the Holy Spirit know and are able to testify we know the Savior lives. Each of us need to be able to declare, as did a prophet of God, even President Kimball, who said:

"Perhaps the most important thing I can say about Jesus Christ, more important than all else I have said, is that he lives. He really does embody all those virtues and attributes the scriptures tell us of. If we can come to know that, we then know the central reality about man and the universe. If we don't accept that truth and that reality, then we will not have the fixed principles or the transcendent truths by which to live out our lives in happiness and in service" ("Jesus: The Perfect Leader," *Ensign,* Aug. 1979, 7).

Many years ago, one of the special witnesses of Christ, Elder Orson F. Whitney of the Quorum of the Twelve, spoke in the

Sunday evening session of the M.I.A. Conference. Early in his address he emphasized the need to know the details about Christ. He said:

> At a time when the Divine character and mission of the world's Redeemer are being questioned, even by many professing Christians, it is a cause for congratulation and rejoicing that there is still found "faith on the earth"—faith in Jesus Christ as the very Son of God, as the virgin-born Savior of mankind, as the anointed and foreordained messenger of Him who "so loved the world, that he gave his only begotten Son, that whosoever believeth in him should not perish, but have everlasting life" (John 3:16).
>
> Among those who hold fast to this conviction, are the Latter-day Saints, or "Mormons." And tonight we unfurl our banner, emblazoned with the slogan of the young men and young women of Zion: *We stand for an individual testimony of the divinity of Jesus Christ.* . . . I know that my Redeemer liveth. Not even Job knew it better. I have evidence that I can not doubt; and this is why I am found among those who tonight unfurl the slogan for which we stand, possessing and proclaiming an individual testimony of the divinity of Jesus Christ (*Improvement Era,* Jan. 1926, 225–26).

Think of the power from on high and the spiritual dignity inherent in our youth and adults alike who have their feet "firmly planted in a divine testimony of the mission of the Lord and Savior, Jesus Christ" and are able to stand as witnesses of the divinity of our beloved Redeemer. Our witness consists not only of a verbal explanation and declaration of the details about Christ, but our very lives also testify of our commitment to what we know. There are details about Christ that, when received and understood, provide us with the power and capacity to defend the divine mission of our Redeemer. These are details that ignite and fan the flames of faith and hope within us. These details assure us of peace in this world and a divine destiny in the world to come.

Hopefully each of us can relate to what Elder Whitney said as a result of our own vision and perspective of the life, mission, and personage of the Savior. Knowing the details about Christ provides the basis for change in all of us. Once we know Him and understand His atoning work, we are never the same again. We are beneficiaries of blessings bestowed upon all who come to Him. We should never lose sight of His primary purpose for coming to the mortal experience. He came to serve as a proxy in the Atonement. His vicarious service extended in two directions. First, He was invested with divine authority to serve as proxy for His Father as He completed the atoning part of the Father's plan of salvation. He did what His Father desired to have done but was unable to do Himself. Secondly, Jesus was proxy for all of us. He vicariously paid the price for our wrongdoings and endured the ordeal of satisfying the demands of justice, that we might obtain the blessings of mercy through His Atonement.

Now, consider that it is in the temples where many Latter-day Saints also have opportunity to serve as proxies in two separate roles. First, we as worthy members can serve as patrons in behalf of deceased persons that they might not any more be deprived of covenant blessings. Secondly, temple workers serve as proxies for the Savior as they perform His sacred priesthood ordinances for those living on both sides of the veil. Vicariously, temple workers are empowered to do what Jesus did for His covenant children in the meridian of time and desires to be done in this dispensation but, logistically, is unable to do Himself. For all who serve as proxy workers or patrons in the temples of our Lord, the words of prayer and testimony contained in a favorite song seem most appropriate to share:

> The King of love my Shepherd is,
> Whose goodness faileth never,
> I nothing lack if I am His,
> And He is mine forever.
> Where streams of living water flow,
> My ransom'd soul He leadeth,
> And where the verdant pastures grow,
> With food celestial feedeth.
>
> Perverse and foolish, oft I stray'd,
> But yet in love He sought me,
> And on His shoulder gently laid,
> And home rejoicing brought me.
>
> In death's dark vale I fear no ill,
> With thee, dear Lord, beside me;
> Thy rod, and staff my comfort still;
> Thy Cross before to guide me.
>
> Thou spread'st a table in my sight,
> Thy unction grace bestoweth,
> And O, the transport of delight
> With which my cup o'erfloweth.
>
> And so, through all the length of days,
> Thy goodness faileth never,

Good Shepherd may I sing Thy praise
Within Thy house forever!
(Harry Rowe Shelley, "The King of Love My Shepherd Is,"
Sing Unto God, 58–63.)

Do the details about Christ really matter? The answer to that question is a resounding YES.

The Savior lives. He died with arms outstretched by nails forcibly positioning Him on a wooden cross. He stands now, voluntarily and lovingly stretching out those same arms to welcome all who will come to Him, a glorified Personage, the Only Begotten Son of God. These are some of the details about Christ that matter. These truths carry a certainty of conviction provided by the comforting and convincing witness of the Holy Spirit to those who seek power from on high.

CHAPTER 6
THE POWER OF COVENANTS

When one of my grandsons turned eight, his mother sat down with him to discuss some of the meaning of his anticipated baptism experience. She explained to him that by being immersed in the water, he would be bearing a testimony to his Heavenly Father that he was entering into a covenant with Him. She asked him if he knew the meaning of the word "covenant." He wasn't sure, but thought maybe it meant that a person makes promises to do certain things.

His mother agreed that a covenant includes making promises, but it is also more. A covenant is not only a promise made by mortals, but includes promises made by the Lord to mortals who keep the conditions of the covenant. Then she said to him, "Now I want you to think seriously about being willing to keep your agreement with the Lord before you decide you are ready to be baptized. If you choose to be baptized, I don't ever want to hear you ask me again, 'Why do we have to go to church?' Just remember you make that decision when you make your covenant with the Lord. Then every time you take the sacrament you will be telling the Lord that you remember your promises and still intend to keep them. Then you can always know that the Lord will keep His promises to you, too."

I thought that little mother did just the right thing in teaching her son about covenants before he made any. It was a simple yet important explanation for that little boy. Without question, all of us need to review the nature of covenants and how to keep them.

Sometimes we use the terms *commitment* or *promise* as though they were synonymous with the word *covenant*. For many people of the world, that may be true. They are meaningful and motivating words of behavior. But a covenant is much more. Covenants come from God by revelation, and the authority to bind man and God in a covenant relationship can only be bestowed by those authorized to represent Him in the performing of covenant-ordinances. No one outside the Lord's church is involved in covenants, though they may very well make various kinds of commitments or promises. Covenants are often mentioned in connection with the words *sacred* or *solemn*. There is a reason. In a revelation warning the Saints in the early days of the Church, the Lord said,

> For this is a day of warning, and not a day of many words. For I, the Lord, am not to be mocked in the last days.
>
> Behold, I am from above, and my power lieth beneath. . . .
>
> Wherefore, let all men beware how they take my name in their lips—
>
> For behold, verily I say, that many there be who are under this condemnation, who use the name of the Lord, and use it in vain, having not authority.
>
> Wherefore, let the church repent of their sins, and I, the Lord, will own them; otherwise they shall be cut off.
>
> Remember that that which cometh from above is sacred, and must be spoken with care, and by constraint of the Spirit; and in this there is no condemnation, and ye receive the Spirit through prayer; wherefore, without this there remaineth condemnation (D&C 63:58–59, 61–64).

Covenants and the authority to create them come from above and are solemnized in the name of the Lord. Therefore, they are sacred and should only be made in solemnity and with sincere intent. Any other intention or deliberate lack of effort to live as promised is a mockery before God. Since such persons bear the Lord's name, it has been used in vain, and the Lord's Spirit departs from them. Consequently, the spiritual power they might have had is missing. They then find themselves under condemnation before the Lord. Speaking of such people, President Spencer W. Kimball stated: "I feel sometimes like severely lecturing men and women who enter into covenants without realizing the nature of the covenants they make, and who use little or no effort to fulfill them" (*The Teachings of Spencer W. Kimball,* 503).

Now, let's focus on a very basic function of Church leaders, whether they be parents, priesthood leaders, or priesthood auxiliary officers. One of the three primary responsibilities of priesthood quorum presidents identified by the Lord is that priesthood quorum presidents are to "teach . . . according to the covenants" (D&C 107:89; see also verses 85–88). Leaders always have two responsibilities relative to covenants:

1. Keep covenants themselves.

2. Teach and assist others to make and keep covenants.

First, how does one keep covenants and faithfully endure to the end? One way of answering that question in principle is found in a statement of the Lord made to Sidney Gilbert: "Behold, I, the Lord, who was crucified for the sins of the world, give unto you a commandment that you shall forsake the world" (D&C 53:2).

When we obtain membership in the Lord's church, we enter into a covenant with Him, we pledge allegiance to Him and His kingdom, and we promise that we will leave behind any worldly thing that would distract us and cause us to detour from the path of righteousness. President David O. McKay taught that the term "world" refers to anyone or anything that is alien or foreign to the Holy Spirit (see CR, Oct. 1911, 58). So for us to forsake the world means that we shun and avoid worldly influences that are out of harmony with and destructive to the Spirit of the Lord. Speaking on this subject, Elder John A. Widtsoe of the Quorum of the Twelve wrote the following:

> All Latter-day Saints enter the new and everlasting covenant when they enter this Church. They covenant to cease sustaining, upholding and cherishing the kingdom of the Devil. . . . They enter the new and everlasting covenant to sustain the Kingdom of God. . . . They take a vow of the most solemn kind, before the heavens and earth, and that, too, upon the validity of their own salvation, that they will sustain truth and righteousness instead of wickedness and falsehood, and build up the Kingdom of God, instead of the kingdoms of this world (*Improvement Era,* June 1945, 349).

It is obvious to all of us that many of the things we confront in this world are spiritually negative influences. Much of the language commonly expressed, a considerable amount of the music performed for listening ears, many of the movies presented to viewing audiences, and many of the dress styles and behavior patterns that are fashionable in our day reflect a prevailing disregard for the spiritual degeneration that precipitates the withdrawal of the Holy Spirit. Compare these worldly lifestyles with the conditions the Lord expects of His covenant people. He revealed "the duty of the members after they are received by baptism" by saying, "The members shall manifest before the church, and also before the elders, by a godly walk and conversation, that they are worthy of it, that there may be works and faith agreeable to the holy scriptures— *walking in holiness before the Lord*" (D&C 20:68–69; emphasis added).

It is manifestly impossible to walk in holiness before the Lord without the edifying presence of the Holy Spirit. Only by the power and influence of spiritual gifts conferred upon covenant people of the Lord can anyone be holy and free from worldly traits and attributes. No one can speak, listen, view, or participate in the ways of the world and still maintain a spiritual attitude of holiness and worthiness. Forsaking the world is not accomplished at some instant in time when making a covenant. That is but the beginning of a lifetime objective of keeping covenants by faithfully striving and enduring to the end in order to ultimately overcome the world and receive the Lord's promised blessings.

Though all of us face unrelenting challenges and temptations, possess wearying weaknesses, and live with an abundance of imperfections, still the Lord provides the encouraging and uplifting strength and power of the Spirit for those who sincerely seek to keep His commandments. The very first covenant we make is created when we are baptized. Included in the Lord's promises to covenant keepers are the words spoken by Alma to those of his people who desired baptism: "Now I say unto you, if this be the desire of your hearts, what have you against being baptized in the name of the Lord, as a witness before him that ye have entered into a covenant with him, that ye will serve him and keep his commandments, *that he may pour out his Spirit more abundantly upon you?*" (Mosiah 18:10; emphasis added).

Because the Lord knows we are too weak and lack the strength to adequately serve Him and keep His commandments by ourselves, He does not leave us alone in our efforts. The Lord promises we shall have the power of His Holy Spirit with all of its gifts and functions. With that power we can not only recognize and resist spirit-leeching activities and forsake them, but we shall also have sufficient power to overcome the world and maintain our sacred covenant-keeping relationship with the Lord.

Tragically, some people have made covenants and then failed to keep them. Two examples will illustrate:

Thomas B. Marsh, President of the First Quorum of Twelve Apostles. After enduring many of the hardships the Saints faced in Missouri, Thomas B. Marsh took a course that led to his excommunication from the Church in 1839. Eighteen years later, he determined he had made serious mistakes and undertook a journey west, hoping to rejoin the Church. In 1857, he knocked on the door of the home of Wandle Mace, a faithful Saint living in Iowa. Brother Mace described him as a broken-down old man he did not recognize, until the man introduced himself as "Thomas B. Marsh, the Mormon apostate" (instead of "the Mormon Apostle," as he previously could have said). He spent the night at the Mace home, where the two men conversed about many of the Church doctrines that were unfamiliar to the former Apostle. He desired baptism, but Brother Mace referred him to the Church authorities who were then living in the West. Thomas Marsh was baptized that same year, and then moved to Ogden, Utah, where he died in 1866 and was buried in obscurity.

James Covill, a former Baptist minister. In 1831, James Covill "covenanted with the Lord that he would obey any command that the Lord would give to him through [Joseph Smith]" (*HC*, 1:143). After receiving a revelation through Joseph Smith, Mr. Covill "rejected the word of the Lord, and returned to his former principles and people" (*HC*, 1:145). In consequence of the broken covenant, the Lord gave a revelation explaining the reasons for Covill's inappropriate behavior. He said, "Behold, verily I say unto you, that the heart of my servant James Covill was right before me, for he covenanted with me that he would obey my word.

"And he received the word with gladness, but straightway Satan tempted him; and the fear of persecution and the cares of the world caused him to reject the word.

"Wherefore he broke my covenant, and *it remaineth with me to do with him as seemeth me good*" (D&C 40:1–3; emphasis added).

We note that Covill's unwise decisions and wrongful behavior are not to be reconciled only with priesthood authorities but, more importantly, with the Lord. It is a serious thing to break covenants with the Lord.

Conversely, we are also aware of so many who have diligently endured great persecutions and much tribulation in consequence of their covenant-making and Church membership, yet, through their possession of power from on high, have remained steadfast and true to their convictions. We mention the following from the experiences of the Saints in Missouri:

Tarring and Feathering of Bishop Partridge. Bishop Edward Partridge and Charles Allen were taken to the public square in Independence and commanded to renounce the Book of Mormon and leave the county. Bishop Partridge said, "I told them that the Saints had suffered persecution in all ages of the world; that I had done nothing which ought to offend anyone; that if they abused me, they would abuse an innocent person; that *I was willing to suffer for the sake of Christ;* but, to leave the country, I was not then willing to consent to it." With this refusal, the men were stripped of their outer clothing, and their bodies were covered with tar and feathers. Bishop Partridge observed, ". . . I was so filled with the Spirit and love of God, that I had no hatred towards my persecutors or anyone else" (*Our Heritage,* 41–42; emphasis added).

Benjamin Johnson at Adam-ondi-Ahman. At age twenty, Benjamin Johnson was arrested and kept under guard for eight days in intensely cold weather before an open campfire. While he was sitting on a log, a "brute" came up to him with a rifle in his hands and said, "You give up Mormonism right now, or I'll shoot you." Benjamin decisively refused, upon which the ruffian took deliberate aim at him and pulled the trigger. The gun failed to discharge. Cursing fearfully, the man declared that he had "used the gun 20 years and it had never before missed fire." Examining the lock, he reprimed the weapon and again aimed and pulled the trigger—without effect. Following the same procedure he tried a third time, but the result was the same. A bystander told him to "fix up his gun a little, then you can kill the cuss all right." So for a fourth and final time the would-be murderer prepared, even putting in a fresh load. However, Benjamin declared, "This time the gun bursted and killed the wretch upon the spot" (*Our Heritage,* 49).

The expulsion of the Saints from Missouri. While their Prophet remained imprisoned, more than 8,000 Saints crossed from Missouri east into Illinois to escape the extermination order of Missouri Governor Lilburn W. Boggs. They were forced to leave in the cold of winter and suffered greatly. The John Hammer family was one of the many families who sought refuge. John recalled the difficult conditions:

Well do I remember the sufferings and cruelties of those days. . . . Our family had one wagon, and one blind horse . . . Into this small wagon we placed our clothes, bedding, some corn meal and what scanty provisions we could muster, and started out into the cold and frost to travel on foot, to eat and sleep by the wayside with the canopy of heaven for a covering. But the biting frosts of those nights and the piercing winds were less barbarous and pitiful than the demons in human form before whose fury we fled. . . . Our family, as well as many others, were almost bare-footed, and some had to wrap their feet in cloths in order to keep them from freezing and protect them from the sharp points of the frozen ground. This, at best, was very imperfect protection, and often the blood from our feet marked the frozen earth. My mother and sister were the only members of our family who had shoes, and these became worn out and almost useless before we reached . . . Illinois (*Our Heritage,* 51–52).

As we observe the faithful Saints who often pay painful prices to be diligent in keeping their covenants, we ask these questions: What is it that creates such conviction and determination in the hearts of untold numbers of souls? Why do some people, all over the world, gather together in the bonds of Church membership and defend, sometimes with their very lives, the truths taught in this Church?

We answer simply for our day. Through the Prophet Joseph Smith, the God of Heaven restored the truths concerning His identity, His nature, and His living reality, and made it possible for all mankind to return to His presence through the atoning sacrifice of His Son Jesus Christ. Those who gain a witness of these restored truths and have a desire to partake of the offered blessings come unto Christ in order to obtain access to Father's eternal kingdom. This process is accomplished through the ordinance of baptism and an accompanying spiritual rebirth by which an eternal covenant is firmly established. Thus, Latter-day Saints are able to develop reservoirs of spiritual strength by virtue of their access to the heavenly powers of the Savior and, through Him, the tender mercies of the Father of us all.

We often reflect on people of previous generations whose covenants were more precious to them than life. Specifically, we might remember "the people of Anti-Nephi-Lehi, who were called the people of Ammon—and they would not take up arms, yea, they had entered into a covenant and they would not break it" (Alma 43:11). These people had been "brought to believe and to know the truth, they were firm, and would suffer even unto death rather than commit sin" (Alma 24:19). They endured, with a hope of spiritual survival, whatever afflictions they faced rather than dishonoring their covenants with God.

But what about us and our day? In many ways, we are a generation like unto the one Joshua addressed when he said, "I have given you a land for which ye did not labour, and cities which ye built not, and ye dwell in them; of the vineyards and oliveyards which ye planted not do ye eat" (Josh. 24:13).

The questions before us include these: Will our children and subsequent posterity look upon our generation with honor and respect as they reflect upon the covenants of their ancestral parents? Will they review our lives and observe in us a dedication and determination to be true to our eternal trusts? Will they see in us a commitment to covenants that is worthy of their emulation? Will their souls be touched and their lives enhanced by the depth of character and conversion that forms their heritage? Will the power born of our faith be sufficiently strong and influential that we will become great ancestors, or will we be only the posterity of great men and women?

Now we turn to the second responsibility of parents and Church leaders. What are the covenants in the Church that we are to teach and help others to make and keep? With the approval of appropriate priesthood authority, Father's children are privileged to receive four different priesthood ordinances that establish and create covenants unto salvation. We are also counseled and regularly permitted to participate in a fifth priesthood ordinance, which renews all previously created covenants. We shall mention each of these and suggest a few thoughts that might be included in the teaching process.

1. Baptism—This is the first priesthood ordinance that establishes covenants for the recipient. Listen to the words of President Kimball:

> Baptism is essential. Jesus Christ . . . traveled to the River Jordan to be baptized by immersion by his cousin John, called the Baptist. By participating in this symbolic ordinance, he demonstrated to all that baptism is the door into this church. . . . To be baptized is to enter into a covenant of commission. But to fail to be baptized when one is convinced the work is divine is a sin of omission (*The Teachings of Spencer W. Kimball*, 110).

This "covenant of commission" includes four specific expectations of covenant makers. (See Mosiah 18:8–10; see also D&C 20:37.) They should:

1. Be desirous of being one of the people of God and of receiving the name of Jesus Christ.

2. Be willing to bear one another's burdens.

3. Stand as a witness of Christ at all times and in all things and in all places.

4. Serve the Lord and keep His commandments.

Consider how intertwined and comprehensive these requirements are. Obviously, anyone who serves the Lord and keeps His commandments will also be a living witness of the Lord's teachings. That same person will be found serving and assisting others in their needs because that is what the Lord's servant people would do. Finally, for a person to appropriately bear the Savior's name, there must be the development of sufficient Christlike attributes in order to know what He would say and do. Then one can think, act, or speak as Jesus would and represent Him as His spokesman and agent; then one will bring honor and glory to His sacred name.

Anyone who complies with these baptismal covenant conditions can expect to be the recipient of the Lord's promised blessings. There are also four of these mentioned:

1. Be redeemed from sin

2. Come forth in the First Resurrection

3. Inherit the blessings of eternal life or exaltation

4. Be blessed with the gifts of the Holy Spirit

The question is sometimes asked, "Does baptism remit sin?" Often there is a split response by those who answer. The accurate answer to the question is a resounding "NO." Baptism does not have the power to remit sin. Our sins can only be remitted by the Savior through the redeeming power of His Atonement (see 2 Ne. 25:26).

As the fourth article of faith states, baptism is *for* the remission of sins. From that same article we note that both faith and repentance precede baptism, and when the individual is thus prepared, he then can worthily be baptized and thus be eligible *for* a remission of his sins. The Lord said to William W. Phelps: "Thou art called and chosen; and *after thou hast been baptized* by water, which if you do with an eye single to my glory [have faith and repent], you shall have a remission of your sins and a reception of the Holy Spirit by the laying on of hands" (D&C 55:1; emphasis added; see also 2 Ne. 31:17).

No one can be redeemed from sin without going to the Savior for that purpose. The Savior declared, "For whoso cometh not unto me is under the bondage of sin" (D&C 84:51). Entering worthily into the baptismal covenant is clearly the qualifier for obtaining the atoning power from on high by which we can be redeemed. We ought not to think or say that people come out of the baptismal water clean from sin, implying that the water has washed away their sins. Baptism is an outward symbol of the cleansing power, but has no inherent power to cleanse or redeem. Obviously, repentance must have been adequately accomplished and precede baptism for the individual to be eligible for a remission of sins that can only be obtained from the Redeemer.

Anyone who is faithful in making and keeping the baptismal covenant will be a partaker of the redeeming power of the Savior's Atonement and will likewise be blessed to receive the fulfillment of the other three promised blessings. For instance, obtaining the outpouring of the power of the Spirit enables one to keep this conditional covenant. A person's capability of being faithful will be increased, and the capacity to resist departures from the Lord's narrow way will be enlarged.

Also of particular interest in this baptismal covenant is the promise of eternal life to the faithful. Eternal life is synonymous with exaltation in the celestial kingdom and requires that a man and woman enter together into the new and everlasting covenant of marriage (see D&C 131:1–4). Those who keep the Lord's commandments as required in the baptismal covenant will most certainly also be worthy of the sealing power in the Lord's law of eternal marriage. Many single Saints have wondered how they could be a candidate for eternal life if they do not have opportunity for a celestial marriage in this life. If they keep their baptismal covenant, they can be content in knowing the Lord will fulfill His promise of exaltation. How and when is not revealed, but there is comfort and peace in knowing all blessings will be bestowed upon covenant-keeping Saints.

2. Melchizedek Priesthood—Another way in which the Lord endows His people with power from on high is the bestowal of the priesthood. Heavenly messengers came to Joseph Smith to ordain him with the authority and power of God, referred to as the priesthood of God. The presence of the priesthood has been perpetuated through the same process since the opening of this dispensation. All worthy adult male members of the Church have opportunity to be ordained with this priesthood, and indeed are required to receive it in order to receive the other two levels of covenant ordinances of the priesthood. This priesthood is received with an oath and covenant described by the Lord in latter-day revelation. (See D&C 84:33–44.) The priesthood holder is expected to comply with two conditions:

1. Live by every word from the mouth of God
2. Magnify one's calling

Keeping the baptismal covenant with respect to being obedient to the Lord's commandments also satisfies this first requirement. It is well to remember that the word that comes "from the mouth of God" comes to us through the scriptures, through utterances of living prophets, and through revelation by the Holy Ghost. In order to live by the word, we must also know what the word is. Incumbent upon us is the responsibility to search, listen to, and be responsive to heavenly sources.

The second condition is that the Lord expects the priesthood holder to magnify his calling. Some do not realize what that calling is, but it can be summed up in one word—*service.* Priesthood holders cannot use the priesthood power and authority in their own behalf. So if they don't use it in service that benefits others, there is little reason for them to hold the priesthood. When a man decides to accept the conditions of this covenant, he, like my grandson, has also determined that he will accept calls and welcome opportunities to serve, whether it be in Church positions, missions, or non-sustained priesthood duties such as home teaching.

Participation in priesthood service is Christlike, for the brethren are doing precisely what the Savior did. His life was one of selfless service and sacrifice without regard to personal convenience or reward, constantly serving others because they had needs, and He could fulfill their needs. Living and doing as He did develops men who are like Him.

As in every covenant, God has promises for the faithful covenant keeper. In the priesthood covenant, the Lord's promises include sanctification by the Spirit, renewed body, seed of Abraham, and all that the Father hath.

To be sanctified by the Spirit requires no plea or even a request. Only worthiness of soul is required, and the cleansing work of the

Holy Spirit is certain. No one could hope for anything greater. He who is sanctified is promised the lifestyle and possessions of the gods and has the undeniable assurance of the blessings described in the inspired writings of the Prophet Joseph Smith, who wrote, "Let virtue garnish thy thoughts unceasingly; then shall thy confidence wax strong in the presence of God; and the doctrine of the priesthood shall distil upon thy soul as the dews from heaven.

"The Holy Ghost shall be thy constant companion, and thy scepter an unchanging scepter of righteousness and truth; and thy dominion shall be an everlasting dominion, and without compulsory means it shall flow unto thee forever and ever" (D&C 121:45–46).

To be promised "all that Father hath" might be the most magnificent declaration ever recorded in holy writ. A marvelous commentary has been written regarding this sublime condition:

> The Lord has promised to all those who are faithful, and who magnify their calling, that they shall be in fellowship with both the Father and the Son, and if they continue faithful, they shall eventually inherit "all that my Father hath." This means that they shall become the sons of God, joint heirs with Jesus Christ, and as expressed in [Doctrine and Covenants] Section 76:55–60, they shall receive the fulness of His glory. When the Lord offers the fulness of his glory on conditions of faithfulness, he attaches a penalty for the breaking of such a glorious and far-reaching covenant. Therefore he has decreed that all those who trample this covenant (which every person receiving the Melchizedek Priesthood receives) under his feet, "and altogether turneth therefrom, shall not have forgiveness of sins in this world nor in the world to come." This means that all who treat

this covenant of the Priesthood with contempt shall never have the privilege of exercising it in the world to come. Therefore they will be barred from celestial exaltation (*Doctrine and Covenants Commentary,* 507).

3. **Endowments**—These covenants can only be received in the temples of the Most High God. Within nine months of the official organization of the Church, the Lord first made mention of a temple (see D&C 36:8), and the following month directed the Saints to move to the first gathering place of this dispensation where, he said, they would "be endowed with power from on high" (D&C 38:32). That place was Kirtland, Ohio, where the first temple was built and initial portions of the endowment ordinance were bestowed. The full endowment ordinance was provided a few years later in Nauvoo, Illinois, and has been administered to the Lord's covenant people ever since. At the time of laying the cornerstone of the Salt Lake Temple on April 6, 1853, President Brigham Young gave a definition of the endowment as follows: "Your endowment is, to receive all those ordinances in the House of the Lord, which are necessary for you, after you have departed this life, to enable you to walk back to the presence of the Father, passing the angels who stand as sentinels, being enabled to give them the key words, the signs and tokens, pertaining to the Holy Priesthood, and gain your eternal exaltation in spite of earth and hell" (*JD,* 2:31).

Speaking of this covenant ordinance known as the temple endowment, Elder James E. Talmage of the Quorum of the Twelve has written the following:

The ordinances of the endowment embody certain obligations on the part of the individual, such as covenant and promise to observe the law of strict virtue and chastity, to be charitable, benevolent, tolerant and pure; to devote both talent and material means to the spread of truth and the uplifting of the race; to maintain devotion to the cause of truth; and to seek in every way to contribute to the great preparation that the earth may be made ready to receive her King,—the Lord Jesus Christ. With the taking of each covenant and the assuming of each obligation a promised blessing is pronounced, contingent upon the faithful observance of the conditions. (*The House of the Lord,* 100).

These sacred ordinances follow the same format as previous covenants. That is, commitments are made to the Lord by the recipients, and blessings are promised by the Lord to the faithful.

4. Eternal or Celestial Marriage—In a statement made to William Clayton, the Prophet Joseph Smith said, "In the celestial glory there are three heavens or degrees;

"And in order to obtain the highest, a man must enter into this order of the priesthood [meaning the new and everlasting covenant of marriage];

"And if he does not, he cannot obtain it.

"He may enter into the other, but that is the end of his kingdom; he cannot have an increase" (D&C 131:1–4).

As with the endowment, the covenants of eternal marriage are to be received only in the temple of the Lord. Therefore, no specific description of the covenant can be provided away from the scene of the sacred ordinance. But Elder Ezra Taft Benson has provided the following valuable observation: "If you are going to be fully happy, you need to be married in the temple of God. Marriage can never mean the same outside the temple as it does inside. It is God's way. You can afford to sacrifice almost anything for that blessing. . . . Temple marriage is a gospel ordinance for exaltation" (*The Teachings of Ezra Taft Benson,* 533–36).

No greater power can be conveyed or acquired than that which is embodied in the promises made to couples who receive and honor their eternal marriage covenants. The Lord revealed some of the magnificent and, for mortals, almost incomprehensible blessings of exaltation. To the faithful, eternally married couples, He described their future and ultimate glorified status:

> Ye shall come forth in the first resurrection . . . and shall inherit thrones, kingdoms, principalities, and powers, dominions, all heights and depths . . . they shall pass by the angels, and the gods . . . to their exaltation and glory in all things, as hath been sealed upon their heads, which glory shall be a fulness and a continuation of the seeds forever and ever.
>
> Then shall they be gods, because they have no end; therefore shall they be from everlasting to everlasting, because they continue; then shall they be above all, because all things are subject unto them. Then shall they be gods, because *they have all power,* and the angels are subject unto them (D&C 132:19–20; emphasis added).

5. Sacrament—As mentioned earlier, partaking of the sacrament is an opportunity to renew our previously made covenants and, among other things, reaffirm our willingness to keep the commandments and bear the name of our Savior. As we take the bread we witness unto God our Father that *we are **willing to** always remember* the Savior. When we take the water, we witness unto God our Father that *we **do** always remember* the Savior. (See D&C

20:77, 79.) Speaking of the sacramental service, President Brigham Young taught, "It is one of the greatest blessings we could enjoy, to come before the Lord and before the angels and before each other, to *witness that we remember* that *the Lord Jesus Christ* has died for us. This proves to the Father that *we remember our covenants,* that we love His gospel, that we love to keep His commandments, and to honor the name of the Lord Jesus upon the earth" (*Latter-day Prophets Speak,* 367; emphasis added).

In return for our observance of and obedience to our renewed covenants, the Lord promises that His Spirit will be with us always. The very presence of the Holy Ghost in our lives is a witness that the covenants we previously made with Him are being kept. We present ourselves before the Lord with the undeniable assurance that all His promises will be fulfilled for our benefit and in our behalf. The words of a sacramental hymn are meaningful to assure us of the bestowal of power as we partake of the sacrament: "In mem'ry of the Crucified, Our Father, we have met this hour. May thy sweet Spirit here abide, *That all may feel its glowing pow'r*" (*Hymns,* no. 190; emphasis added).

It is hoped that each of us may seek the security and peace of God-given covenants made and kept. As we live close to the compelling influence of the Holy Spirit, we can utilize the uplifting power that comes from on high that we need in order to be faithful covenant members of the Lord's kingdom. How marvelous it would be for us to be described as were faithful Lamanites of old:

> . . . the church was broken up in all the land save it were among a few of the Lamanites who were converted unto the true faith; and they would not depart from it, for they were firm, and steadfast, and immovable, willing with all

diligence to keep the commandments of the Lord (3 Ne. 6:14).

Nephi saw in vision the conditions existing upon the earth in our day, in our dispensation:

And it came to pass that I, Nephi, beheld *the power* of the Lamb of God, that it *descended upon the saints* of the church of the Lamb, and upon *the covenant people of the Lord,* who were scattered upon all the face of the earth; and they were *armed with righteousness and with the power of God* in great glory (1 Ne. 14:14; emphasis added).

May the prayerful and inspired petition of the Prophet Joseph Smith burn within our hearts and be repeated as our own prayerful expression of our deepest desires: "Put upon thy servants the testimony of the covenant" (D&C 109:38).

CHAPTER 7
THE POWER OF THE ONLY SURE AND
SAFE FOUNDATION

We live in a time of political, economic, physical, and spiritual unrest. Multitudes of people live in fear. They are asking questions, seeking direction, and struggling for strength to bear burdensome afflictions. For various reasons, peoples' lives have been drastically disrupted. For many, concern has replaced comfort, and security has given way to anxiety. The pollster George Gallup Jr. made the following observation: "People are reaching out in all directions in their attempt to escape from the *seen* world to the *unseen* world. There is a deep desire for spiritual moorings—a hunger for God" (*U.S. News & World Report*, May 6, 2002, 42).

People are in need of powers beyond their own that will provide them with firm anchors to which they can cling. Drifting without direction develops desperation. Only God's power from on high satisfies the hunger for spiritual moorings. To discover and obtain it depends on the structures of life we seek to build.

One of the challenges of our lives is to maintain spiritual equilibrium while responding to the many requests or responsibilities requiring our time, talents, or resources. Some involvements are self-imposed, while others may be unforeseen opportunities or even results of unfortunate happenings.

When we design careers or set a course to develop our skills or talents we, at the same time, predetermine the use of considerable amounts of time and energy. We create commitments and dedicate our diligence in anticipation of our framework of life that lies ahead.

Elder Neal A. Maxwell provided some cautionary counsel on these matters:

> Those who are high achievers and highly devoted to their secular specialty—but often to the exclusion of God—nevertheless display a commendable and beneficial discipline in that thing, bringing them success and blessing others. Their egos can facilitate unusual achievement, but the challenge of bypassing spiritual submissiveness must be paid.
>
> It happens if our hobbies and specialties become obsessions performed to the exclusion of worship of God. Then there is no way—however well we keep the other commandments—that we can truly keep the first commandment: worshiping Him with all our hearts and minds. Nevertheless, though the contribution made by such sincere individuals may still benefit many, it keeps such individuals from coming off conqueror in the real contest of life (see D&C 10:5) (*Moving in His Majesty and Power*, 84–85).

It is incumbent upon all of us to determine upon what foundations we will choose to build and structure our lives. Thankfully, we are free to decide the degree to which our personal interests, gifts, talents, and opportunities will be used to determine the focus of our lives. Unfortunately, some of us sometimes develop tunnel vision and lose perspective. Perhaps a few examples might illustrate how some people, without the clear views provided by the power of the Holy Spirit, mistakenly seek satisfaction by immersion in temporal or temporary matters only.

Most of us have known individuals who build solely on a foundation of academic attainment. They may make the assumption that enviable scholastic honors and recognition justify an exclusion of effort to develop structural strength on any other foundation. Any other demand on their time may be viewed as an interference with the acquisition of various levels of educational certifications. Without an accompanying balance of spiritual emphasis, this kind of narrow focus and thinking leaves a person without the benefit of spiritual power from on high.

Some people focus on gaining appointments to positions of prestige or on acquiring monetary wealth. Some even seek tenaciously to build on a foundation of monetary assets for themselves with little regard for others who may be professionally, financially, or socially injured as a result of their self-centered quest. In contrast, many others with wealth selflessly share what they have obtained and provide humanitarian assistance and charitable contributions to worthy causes and people in need. Commendably, this latter group pursues the patterns prescribed by the greatest Servant of all with an accompanying presence of spiritual motivation and strength.

Students who struggle financially while seeking to reach educational goals, young married couples beginning family life with precious little of this world's goods, employees on meager salaries barely making ends meet—all of these can identify with the desire to eventually obtain financial independence. Some might even dream of a day when they can leave the work force and just rest in the lap of luxury. But what might be the cost of an obsession with economic objectives alone? How much is it really worth to obtain the world and lose relationships, either with God, family, or friends? An interesting insight was provided in an article written by two ministers serving in New York State:

> We once heard of a CEO who spoke at his retirement dinner to a group of young executives. He said, "I know you want my job, and I'll tell you how to get it. Last week my daughter was married, and as she walked down the aisle, I realized I did not know the name of her best friend, or the last book she read, or her favorite color. That's the price I paid for this job. If you want to pay that price, you can have it" ("How Do You Find God," *Reader's Digest,* Apr. 2002, 97–98).

Some young people focus on the development of athletic abilities and seek to build on a limited foundation of athletic opportunities with varying levels of accompanying rewards. They see and hear of talented athletes who demonstrate their special skills under competitive conditions. Almost unimaginable amounts of money are proffered to professional athletes, vast audiences applaud their accomplishments, their names are commonly mentioned in casual conversations, and their images are sometimes projected to countless viewers worldwide. Some of these talented athletes are recipients of accolades and adulation that might better be reserved for more deserving examples of legitimate heroes. Because of their popularity, they become advertising spokespersons and role models in social, educational, and professional environments. Sometimes emulation of athletes even extends to mimicking certain dimensions of their personal lives that are not exemplary or praiseworthy, but serve instead as unstable foundations, creating an inappropriate influence on unwary or unthinking youth.

Many other people are spectators, and some even become obsessed observers of sporting activities and—often at the expense of personal, family, or even spiritual activities—spend an inordinate amount of time and resources viewing, reading, and discussing current sporting events. Reason dictates that extending one's involvement in an overabundance of sporting activity is likely to result in a restriction of the flow of spiritual power.

Certain other people effectively develop their talents and structure their lives on a foundation of music alone. Either by performing, teaching, or by some other meaningful way, they provide stimulating musical experiences for the edification and enjoyment of themselves and others. Such artists bless the lives of many as they share their natural and developed talents. But wisdom warns that their lives should not be so narrowly focused that they fail to frame another more essential structure on a more sure and eternal foundation.

These and many other endeavors and objectives may well be worthy of diligent efforts and dedicated commitments. But a legitimate and scriptural concern is that they must not be the weightiest matters of our mortal lives. They must not be at the top of our list of priorities. Rather, they should be secondary supplements to our personal adherence to divine directives that more accurately define proper perspectives.

Listen to the words of Helaman, as he counseled his sons on this critical issue: "And now, my sons, remember, remember that it is upon the rock of our Redeemer, who is Christ, the Son of God, that ye must *build your foundation;* that when the devil shall send forth his mighty winds, yea, his shafts in the whirlwind, yea, when all his hail and his mighty storm shall beat upon you, it shall have no power over you to drag you down to the gulf of misery and endless wo, because of the rock upon which ye are built, *which is a sure foundation,* a foundation whereon if men build *they cannot fall*" (Hel. 5:12; emphasis added).

None of us want to fall or fail. So it behooves us to obtain the spiritually protective powers resulting from building on the rock of our Redeemer as the only sure and safe foundation. How to do so is clear. The way to build on the Savior's sure foundation is to develop a faith and trust in His words and live in harmony with His teachings. We are then certain of protection from the deceptive and spiritually destructive powers of the adversary. Consider a few examples of this eternal principle.

One day a young woman came to my office wanting help with a problem. I asked what it was. She said she was pregnant but not married. Furthermore, she did not want to be pregnant or married. She wanted an abortion. She claimed to have prayed a lot about what she should do, but didn't seem to get any answers to her prayers. I told her the answer to her prayer was in my file cabinet. I took out a statement by the First Presidency and read to her what the Lord thinks about His children aborting their children. The Lord had already revealed through His prophet the position of heaven on that subject. All she needed to do was to trust Him and thereby avoid the resultant regret and sorrow that always accompanies decisions that conflict with the Lord's teaching. When she finally decided to trust the Lord's wisdom, she began at that same moment to build on the only sure and safe foundation. Heavenly direction provided personal power to do the right thing.

On another occasion, a young man wanted to talk with me about whether he should go on a mission. His girlfriend didn't want him to go, suggesting instead that they should be married and after they retired they could then serve a mission together. She insisted that it would be selfish of him to go without her, and if he did, such a decision would mean he didn't really love her and she wouldn't wait for him. He thought that he loved the girl and just couldn't decide what he should do. I told him the Lord had already declared through a latter-day Apostle and prophet that "every young man is as much obligated to go on a mission as he is to pay his tithing, attend his meetings, keep the Sabbath day holy, and keep his life spotless and clean" (Elder Spencer W. Kimball, "Address to Seminary and Institute Faculty," Brigham Young University, June 28, 1968). To build his life on a sure and safe foundation, this young man would need to trust the Lord's judgment, faithfully serve his mission, and ignore any opinion that would persuade him to go contrary to divine counsel. He subsequently told the girl he was determined to follow prophetic counsel and would be going on a mission. He hoped she could support that decision because he would only marry a girl who honored those same commitments. He had the power from on high to withstand opposing opinions.

A Jewish woman had studied the gospel of Jesus Christ and struggled with the decision of whether she should join the Church. After considerable pondering and praying, she was converted to the Lord, baptized into His church, and then wrote the following summary of her experience: "There are times when people feel that the best advice is to listen to their own inner voice, moving with it as they are led by it, forgetting that their own reasoning is not a divine voice and can never be a safe guide to behavior. Human reason is only what we have accumulated in knowledge about our morals and our choices. Even with experience of life, reason alone is never enough to guide us. We need divine help . . ." ("Notes of a Jewish Convert to the LDS Church," *Best Books Digest,* 3). She discovered the value of trusting the divine voice as the only way she could build on a sure foundation.

Sometimes we forget to apply this principle when we wrestle with some of the common problems we all encounter while striving to keep our covenants and be worthy in the sight of the Lord. Here are four examples of challenging questions:

1. How do we decide whether to participate in work or recreational activities on the Sabbath or to worship the Lord and keep the Sabbath day holy?

2. How do we decide whether to pay bills or tithing when there doesn't appear to be enough money to do both?

3. How do we decide whether to view certain videos or movies when there is objectionable material in them?

4. How do students decide whether to be honest in exams and assignments when there is pressure to perform well and an opportunity to obtain information inappropriately?

We will always be found building on a sure foundation if we simply determine the will of the Lord on these matters and then make His will our own. Listen to the promises made to those who trust in the Lord as Alma bore his testimony to his son Helaman. He said, "I do know that whosoever shall put their trust in God shall be supported in their trials, and their troubles, and their afflictions, and shall be lifted up at the last day" (Alma 36:3).

Some years ago, a dear friend called me at my office and asked if I would give him a blessing the next time I came to his area. We made arrangements to meet, and then he told me what his need was. His wife was suffering with a terminal illness and he needed to know from the Lord what kind of faith he needed to have. He wondered if he should seek to develop sufficient faith to extend to his wife a healing blessing through the administration of a priesthood blessing. Or, if she was not to be healed, he would seek faith to accept the Lord's decision, plead for strength to comfort her, and provide whatever assistance she needed to get through the illness. Either way he would trust the Lord's will—he just needed to know what it was. Though the Lord did not provide for a healing blessing to be given, this brother was truly anchored on a safe foundation. I am a witness that he subsequently received the support Alma promised.

There is an account in the Book of Mormon of the Nephite armies marching against a vastly greater Lamanite force who were entrenched in cities built by the Nephites and previously fortified by them. Though they faced overwhelming odds, still the Nephites confronted their enemies with unwavering confidence in a favorable outcome. Why? Listen to their own words of explanation: "We trust in our God. . . . We trust God will deliver us, notwithstanding the weakness of our armies, yea, and deliver us out of the hands of our enemies" (Alma 58:33, 37).

Like these Nephites, many of us have faced challenges and made difficult decisions that dealt with life-altering or even life-threatening consequences. Though we often don't see how favorable results can be obtained, we should remember to build on the only sure foundation by following the only safe course: *Trust the Lord.*

I am remembering a wonderful Latter-day Saint woman who came seeking the Lord's counsel through a priesthood blessing. She explained that she was happily expecting her third or fourth child but had been told by three different doctors that because of unsafe conditions that were developing in her pregnancy, she must abort her baby. She was told that failure to do so right away would most certainly result in the death of her unborn child anyway, and most likely would take her life as well. After explaining why she had come to receive a priesthood blessing, she made the following statement: "God himself would have to tell me to destroy this baby before I would do it." The blessing was pronounced.

Several months later, I was seated on the stand in a ward fast and testimony meeting. I watched, and wept, as this mother placed her baby in the arms of her faithful priesthood husband, who then gave that precious infant child a name and a father's blessing. Would anyone suppose she will ever regret having trusted God, followed His foundation-based counsel, and then obtained the life-saving powers of heaven?

There is another matter that has attracted the feelings of my heart. Many single adults in the Church have despaired because they have not had opportunity to marry and be sealed to a worthy spouse for time and eternity. Though they live worthy lives, many feel they have been forgotten, or that the Lord has failed to provide them the opportunity to experience family relationships with companions and children. Some of them think of themselves as second-class citizens in the Lord's kingdom and sometimes resent hearing sermons or testimonies on the subject of eternal families. They wonder how they can ever hope to enjoy the fullness of the gospel blessings.

Similarly, some marriage partners find themselves alone in their faithful efforts to keep their marriage covenants. Though they personally strive to maintain the Lord's standards of celestial marriage, their companion may fail to live the covenants upon which eternal blessings are predicated. Under these circumstances the faithful spouse may lose hope of ever receiving the glorious blessings promised at the sacred marriage altar.

We may not see how such problems can possibly be resolved. It would be well for these dear Saints to be reminded of the Lord's promise of eternal life to all who keep baptismal covenants (see Mosiah 18:9). Since eternal life, or exaltation, cannot be obtained without entering into and keeping eternal marriage covenants, we may wonder how such blessings can be provided. But it was the

Lord who made that promise to His worthy and faithful covenant children. Trust Him to keep His covenant if we keep ours. How or when the promises unfold may not be apparent now. But we do know that all faithful Saints who build on that sure foundation have access to heavenly powers and are safe in their anticipation of being glorified with their own loving family members throughout all eternity.

Sometimes the Lord's blessings are delayed until and unless we first do what we can do. Divine intervention seldom precedes the fulfillment of our duties and responsibilities. Rather, the bestowal of blessings commonly accompanies our own efforts to accomplish worthy goals.

Many remember Nephi's testimony when he said: ". . . we know that it is by grace that we are saved, *after all we can do*" (2 Ne. 25:23; emphasis added).

Among other things, that statement tells us that we must put forth our best effort (coupled with the Lord's help) in doing what we can to bring about righteous results. Only then can we expect the Lord to extend His additional powers and influence in providing desired blessings. First we determine to trust Him; then we heed and obey His counsel. We do what we can do with confidence that He will honor the promises He has made to us.

Many years ago, a bishop friend of mine took a group of Scouts on a camping trip in Yellowstone Park for several days. They traveled in canoes across a very large lake to get to their camp area on its far shore. After being there a few days, they heard a radio message warning campers of an early-season storm moving into the area. It would bring snow and cold temperatures. The bishop decided they should cut their camping trip short and prepare to leave for home the next morning. However, by morning, the winds preceding the storm had already come and were creating very dangerous water conditions on the lake, especially for young boys in canoes.

The bishop delayed their departure, hoping the wind would calm down. He went into the woods two or three times to plead for the Lord to calm the winds. While pleading for this blessing, the bishop received a very distinct impression from the Lord. It was simply, "Bishop, what are you waiting for?"

He knew what to do. He loaded the boys and their camp equipment into the canoes and pushed the canoes out into the wind-whipped water. As they left the safety of the shore, the wind ceased to blow, the air was still, and the water became calm. After crossing the lake and arriving safely on the other side, they all knelt to thank the Lord for His miraculous assistance. Each of them learned a valuable lesson. Though we trust in the Lord, He expects us to move ahead and take steps in the right direction before His blessing is bestowed. There wasn't any reason for the Lord to calm the wind on the lake while they were still sitting on the shore. The power from on high that controlled the elements was predicated on the faith and works of the petitioners.

While explaining three interrelating elements of faith that make possible the acquisition of heavenly powers, Elder David A. Bednar taught:

We find a powerful example of the interaction among assurance, action, and evidence as the children of Israel transported the ark of the covenant under the leadership of Joshua (see Joshua 3:7–17). Recall how the Israelites came to the river Jordan and were promised the waters would part, and they would be able to cross over on dry ground. Interestingly, the waters did not part as the children of Israel stood on the banks of the river waiting for something to happen; rather, the soles of their feet were wet before the water parted. The faith of the Israelites was manifested in the fact that they walked into the water *before* it parted. They walked into the river Jordan with a future-facing assurance of things hoped for [acquisition of power from on high]. As the Israelites moved forward, the water parted, and as they crossed over on dry land, they looked back and beheld the evidence of things not seen. In this episode, faith as assurance led to action and produced the evidence of things not seen that were true ("Seek Learning By Faith," *Ensign,* Sept. 2007, 63).

The Book of Mormon prophet Jacob described the efforts of the Nephites as they sought to protect their people from their Lamanite enemies. Note how they first fulfilled their responsibilities while they built on a sure foundation of trust in their God. Jacob recorded: "Wherefore, the people of Nephi did fortify against [the Lamanites] with their arms, and with all their might, *trusting in the God and rock of their salvation;* wherefore, they became as yet, conquerors of their enemies" (Jacob 7:25; emphasis added).

I think of a saintly sister who once told me of her mother's experience as a young girl in Switzerland before her family immigrated to America in the late 1800s. The family had joined the Church and decided to come to Utah where they could mingle with the Saints and be close to the prophet. As a result of their decisions, they experienced a great deal of persecution from the people who lived in their small town.

The night before their planned departure, the young daughter was walking alone up the hill to her home. As she walked by two men who were working alongside the road, she overheard one of them say, "Isn't that the Mormon girl that is leaving tomorrow?

She's alone and we can easily catch her." She began to run, but she could tell they were running faster and would catch her long before she could reach her home. As she ran, she poured out her heart to Heavenly Father, telling him that she had always kept herself pure and begging him to help her escape from the men who were coming after her.

In an instant, she was standing alone on the front porch of her home. She did not know how she got there, but she knew some power had done for her what she could not have done for herself. As Helaman had promised his sons, this young woman found that building on the Lord's sure foundation brought her a literal escape from the powers of the adversary. She, like Jacob's people, found that a life of trusting in God made possible the conquering of her enemies.

Frequently in our society, controversial issues arise that invoke questions concerning the Church. With regularity, people in and out of the Church can be heard to criticize the Church by saying, "The Church is out of line," or they refer to the Church doctrine on some subject as being too strict. It seems the real problem is a lack of trust in God. Instead of speaking of Church doctrine, it should be called the *Lord's* doctrine. The Church's position on a matter would be better described as the *Lord's* position. Then it becomes clear that one must take a stand either in favor of or in opposition to the Lord. Should we not be wise and build our trust on the rock of Christ, the one sure foundation?

Now, may we refer back to the four questions raised earlier, and take note of statements from the Lord's anointed servants. We are then free to determine our own level of trust.

1. How do we decide whether to participate in work or recreational activities on the Sabbath or to worship the Lord and keep

the Sabbath day holy?

The First Presidency:

We sense that many Latter-day Saints have become lax in their observance of the Sabbath day. We should refrain from shopping on the Sabbath and participating in other commercial and sporting activities that now commonly desecrate the Sabbath.

We urge all Latter-day Saints to set this holy day apart from activities of the world and consecrate themselves by entering into a spirit of worship, thanksgiving, service, and family-centered activities appropriate to the Sabbath. As Church members endeavor to make their Sabbath activities compatible with the intent and Spirit of the Lord, their lives will be filled with joy and peace (First Presidency Letter, Sept. 28, 1992).

2. How do we decide whether to pay bills or tithing when there doesn't appear to be enough money to do both?

Elder George Q. Morris, Assistant to the Quorum of Twelve:

I think when people say they haven't money enough to pay tithing, they should say they haven't faith enough to pay tithing. It is my conviction that we pay tithing with faith and not with money (CR, Apr. 1953, 111).

President Joseph F. Smith:

By this principle [of tithing] the loyalty of the people of this Church shall be put to the test. By this principle it shall be known who is for the kingdom of God and who is against it. By this principle it shall be seen whose hearts are set on doing the will of God and keeping His commandments . . . by it it shall be known whether we are faithful or unfaithful. In this respect, it is as essential as faith in God, as repentance of sin, as baptism for the remission of sin, or as the laying on of hands for the gift of the Holy Ghost (CR, Apr. 1900, 47).

3. How do we decide whether to view certain videos or movies when there is objectionable material in them?
President Ezra Taft Benson:

Consider carefully the words of the prophet Alma to his errant son, Corianton, "Forsake your sins, and go no more after the lusts of your eyes" (Alma 39:9). The lusts of your eyes. In our day, what does that expression mean? Movies, television programs, and video recordings that are both suggestive and lewd. Magazines and books that are obscene and pornographic. We counsel you . . . not to pollute your minds with such degrading matter, for the mind through which this filth passes is never the same afterward. Don't . . . participate in any entertainment that is immoral, suggestive, or pornographic. Don't listen to music that is degrading (CR, Apr. 1986, 58).

4. How do students decide whether to be honest in exams and assignments when there is pressure to perform well and an opportunity to obtain information inappropriately?
President Gordon B. Hinckley:

Simple honesty is so remarkable a quality. It is of the very essence of integrity. It demands that we be straightforward, unequivocal, in walking the straight and narrow line of what is right and true. It is so easy to cheat. At times it is so enticing to do so. Better a poor grade than a dishonest act (*BYU Speeches of the Year,* Oct. 17, 1995, 53).

Might each of us remember, with King Mosiah, that the Lord extends His arms of mercy to those who put their trust in Him (see Mosiah 29:20). Who amongst us does not need an extension of His mercy? Those arms are real. They are extended in welcoming each one who has trusted Him and has built upon the rock of His sure foundation. As each day of our lives comes to a close may we reflect upon our life that day and, as we kneel in benediction before the Lord, raise our voices and declare as Nephi when he said, "O Lord, I have trusted in thee" (2 Ne. 4: 34).

Though the world around us is in a terrible state of strife and turmoil, we all still desire peace. The world at large cannot currently experience peace, but individually we can. We can obtain it the same way the Prince of Peace did. And what was that way? One of the greatest tributes ever paid to Jesus by mortal man was inadvertently declared by His mocking and reviling enemies as He hung on the cross in the closing moments of his atoning sacrifice. They said, "He trusted in God" (Matt. 27:43). May we build on that same sure and safe foundation, that we might access and be blessed by power from on high.

CHAPTER 8

THE POWER OF THE SPIRIT—
THE GIFT OF GREAT WORTH

Over the years, we have all frequently heard people speak of being aware of the presence of the Holy Spirit; often, they mention how strong it seemed to be at the time. That experience may take place in meetings or while reading scriptures or while listening to a spiritual message or under many other circumstances. We may feel it in the presence of individuals who seem to radiate a spiritual countenance, and often we notice it when entering a special place that seems to enclose a spiritual power. For instance, when the Lord revealed the dedicatory prayer for the Kirtland Temple, He said that "all people who shall enter upon the threshold of the Lord's house may *feel thy power*" (D&C 109:13; emphasis added). The value of those feelings cannot be determined; there is no way to measure that. Rather, the value is measured by its worth to the individual recipient. A university economics professor taught that the worth of anything depends on how much a person is willing to give up to obtain it. That is a business principle, but it is appropriate for our use in other ways as well.

Most of us have heard the story of the Prophet Joseph Smith going to Washington to meet with the president of the United States, who asked him how our religion differs from all the others. His answer essentially was that we have the gift of the Holy Ghost (see *HC*, 4:42). Although we may all be familiar with that reply, perhaps we still need to catch more of the significance of it.

Sometime after his death, Joseph Smith made a visit to Brigham Young. President Young recorded:

> [The Prophet Joseph] said, "Tell the people to be humble and faithful and be sure to keep the Spirit of the Lord. It will lead them right. Be careful and not turn away the still small voice; it will teach you what to do and where to go; it will yield the fruits of the kingdom. Tell the brethren to keep their hearts open to conviction, so that when the Holy Ghost comes to them, their hearts will be ready to receive it. They can tell the Spirit of the Lord from all other spirits; it will whisper peace and joy to their souls; it will take the malice, hatred, strife, and all evil from their hearts; and their whole desire will be to do good, to bring forth right-eousness and to build up the kingdom of God. Tell the brethren if they will follow the Spirit of the Lord they will go right" (*Manuscript History of Brigham Young 1846–1847,* 529–530).

It is interesting that Brigham Young appeared after his death to Wilford Woodruff and repeated much of that same message. He reaffirmed the need to "teach the people . . . that they must labor and so live as to obtain the Holy Spirit, for without this you cannot build up the kingdom; without the spirit of God you are in danger of walking in the dark, and in danger of failing to accomplish your calling" (*Discourses of Wilford Woodruff,* 290).

That gift, which has been emphasized by prophets, is a meaningful and identifiable part of the Latter-day Saint environment. It is the unique distinction identified by Joseph Smith in his response to the president of the United States as mentioned earlier, and fills at least three major needs for us. I would like to address each of those.

First, we need to know what is true and right. Second, we need to *desire* to do what is right. Third, we need to have the *strength* or capacity to do what is right.

KNOWING WHAT IS RIGHT

In D&C 91:4 we read of the Lord's instructions to the Prophet Joseph on the subject of the Apocrypha. Joseph was reminded that "the Spirit manifesteth truth." Or, as Nephi wrote in his last recorded message, "The Holy Ghost . . . will show unto you all things what ye should do" (2 Ne. 32:5). If we know something is of the Lord, then we know it is true, and we must know it is true in order to exercise faith in it. Faith can only be exercised in that which is not seen but is true (see Alma 32:21), and the Holy Ghost is the testator of truth (see John 15:26; 16:13).

By ourselves we cannot always know what is true or what is right. Every General Authority thinks of that when he has the assignment to reorganize a stake presidency. He has to learn who the Lord has chosen to be the new stake president. It is difficult to be among so many strangers and expect to find the right man. How can one ever hope to know whom the Lord has chosen? That particular process of decision making always weighs heavily on the heart of the responsible authority. It is interesting that the Lord makes the choice, though previously unknown to the presiding authority, and yet sometimes the man whom he has chosen already knows through the impressions of the Holy Spirit.

On one occasion, I sat at the side of an Apostle for many hours as we interviewed various brethren in a stake. At the conclusion of those interviews, the member of the Twelve turned to me and said,

"Have you seen or met the new stake president yet?" That was a tough question, but I was able to answer in the affirmative. "Who is it?" he asked. I had hoped he would make the decision and only ask me for support, but he was asking me to speak first.

I told him what I thought and how I felt and then waited for his response. He told me I was right. I asked him how long he had known. He said, "Since we first met him." It had taken me considerably longer. The Spirit had pointed out the man. As the call was extended to the brother, we learned that the Holy Spirit had already told him several days earlier. The Lord never makes a mistake. The Spirit always lets us know what we should do. It always tells us what is right.

Many years ago I was teaching a night class at Brigham Young University. A young mother who was a student in that class shared with me her experience. While sitting in the class, she had an impression come to her mind that she should go home. She looked at the clock and realized the class would not be over for another twenty-five minutes and thought it would be rude for her to leave. She decided to wait for the class to be excused. In another instant the Spirit whispered to her to go home immediately. She quietly left the classroom. Driving into her neighborhood, she felt the urgency of being there. She drove up in front of her home just in time to see her one-year-old toddler step off the curb into the road with cars coming and going. Somehow he had escaped from the babysitter. Of course, the mother did not know what other ending there might have been to that story, but the Lord knew she needed to be home. The Spirit tells us what we should do.

As the mission president in the Louisiana Baton Rouge Mission, I struggled to know each time new missionaries arrived as to where and with whom they should be assigned. On one occasion, I sat pondering in my office in the mission home, after interviewing all the new missionaries. The next morning it would be my responsibility to announce the assignments for all of them. An older couple had come with this group, and I felt impressed to send them to Poplarville, Mississippi. I had not been to Poplarville at that time, but I knew about the very small branch of the Church that was there. I wrote the notation on their assignment letter and went to bed.

The following morning, after we had spent some orientation time with the new missionaries, the telephone rang in the mission office. The caller was the branch president in Poplarville, Mississippi, who said he had just learned from his doctor that he must have immediate surgery. He was leaving for Jackson, Mississippi, that afternoon and wondered if it would be possible to send a missionary couple to the branch to take over the duties of the branch presidency while he would be gone for the next several weeks. I would not have known how to create an extra missionary couple when all of the ones we had were already assigned elsewhere in the mission. I told the branch president that had he called twenty-four hours earlier, I don't know what we could have done. But a couple had arrived the day before who had already been assigned to that branch. Obviously, the Lord knew of the need, though I surely did not.

I often think of the need for the Spirit. Before there was a church in our dispensation, the Lord told Hyrum Smith that he was to seek to obtain the word of the Lord. Then the Lord promised Hyrum he would have **the power of the Spirit unto the convincing of men** (see D&C 11:21). Many people have had the gospel preached to them by missionaries and members, but were not convinced of the truthfulness of the message. Missionaries, teachers, or even prophets do not have convincing power. But the Holy Spirit comes from on high and He does have that power. Only by that Spirit do we really know and really become convinced of what is right and what we should do.

Interesting things happen when the Spirit works on people. Two elders were driving down a street in New Orleans, Louisiana, on their way to an appointment. The elder who was not driving, who probably had his mind more on the things of the Spirit than did the driver, told his companion that he felt they should go see a Mrs. Garcia. The companion reminded him that they had seen her the night before and that they had an appointment with someone else and were almost late. The first elder said, "I know, but I think we should go see her again. Would it be all right if we go there instead?" His companion turned the car around, went back to the home of Mrs. Garcia, and knocked on her door.

When Mrs. Garcia came to the door and saw the elders, she began to cry and invited them in. She then explained to the elders that she hadn't slept a wink since they left the night before. That had been their first visit to her, and they had introduced her to the Book of Mormon, a testimony of Jesus Christ. She had never heard of it before but had spent the night reading it and asking the Lord if it was true. She kept feeling it must be true, but then she would have doubts and fears and would wonder if maybe it wasn't true. The nagging feelings persisted. She enjoyed reading the book and went back to the pages to read the words again and again. Each time she did, she felt good and somehow seemed to know that it was true. Then came the doubts again, and it went like that all night.

Finally, she could stand it no longer. She knelt down at the side of her bed and said, "Oh, dear Heavenly Father, I have to know if this is true. If this book is true and if the message is true, please send those elders back to me that I might know." As she finished her prayer, she heard a knock on the door and found the elders standing there.

DESIRING TO DO RIGHT

To have a desire to do what is right, we need the Spirit. As recorded in the twenty-eighth chapter of Mosiah, the sons of King Mosiah, as converted young men, were anxious to go to the Lamanites and share the message of the gospel with them. The Lamanites did not understand the benefits and values of the gospel and were enemies to the Nephites. Yet these young men desired to go and proclaim the gospel to them. They trembled at the thought that any human soul should perish without the gospel of Jesus Christ. They inquired of their father, the king, asking permission to go into a politically and religiously opposed environment. Arrangements were made and approval was given. Interestingly enough, this statement appears in the fourth verse: "Thus did the Spirit of the Lord work upon them."

That desire to do what is right comes from within and is created by the Spirit. No wonder the Prophet Joseph Smith, President Brigham Young, and President Wilford Woodruff emphasized so strongly the need for the people to receive the Spirit. It is not enough to *know* what is right. We must also desire to *do* what is right. The desire to do so is created and strengthened as we allow the Spirit to work upon us.

In an interview, a brother shared with me an experience two young missionaries had with the Spirit. The elders were struggling to learn a new language. Though they had not become proficient in speaking it, they were trying. They were doing all they could but still could not communicate very well. One day they attempted to teach a discussion to a man in the foreign language. He was enthralled with their message and invited them back. Again, he listened intently, and at the end of their message, he asked them to come back. When they returned, the man listened and invited them to return again. After four or five of these visits, the man said to the elders, "It has been wonderful to have you come. I have not understood what you have said; your language is not very good. But I know by how I feel that what you said is true. Whatever I have to do to be a part of what you have, I will do." The man then asked them to send someone to teach him who could speak well enough for him to understand the message, though he already knew it was true.

The Spirit has the power to tell us what we should do and to give us the desire to do it. Man does not have that kind of power. It is not of man; it comes from on high.

While I was serving as a mission president, a General Authority toured our mission. As I sat in one zone conference with him, he leaned over to me and asked what was wrong with a particular elder that he identified to me. I inquired why he asked, and he responded, "Because he has a dark countenance." The missionary was a total stranger, but a representative of the Lord recognized the absence of the Spirit. I told him the elder was the one I had spoken to him about earlier who was having trouble and would need to be sent home.

There are things that all of us might do that would cause us to lose the Spirit. Without it we don't really desire to do what is right. Without that desire, we will likely accept one or more of the many invitations we receive to do what is wrong. That elder had yielded to suggestions of behavior that were incompatible with the responsibilities and standards of a missionary. His dark countenance reflected his lack of desire that would have motivated righteous behavior had he been susceptible to the persuasions of the Spirit.

Strength to Do Right

I have thought about the need to have the Spirit to develop the capacity to do what is right. Consider the statement of Nephi that when a person speaks by the power of the Holy Ghost the power of the Spirit carries the message unto the heart (see 2 Ne. 33:1). He did not say *into* the heart because it can't always get in. It can only enter if the heart is not hardened against the Holy Spirit as described in the next verse: "But behold, there are many that harden their hearts against the Holy Spirit, that it hath no place in them; wherefore, they cast many things away which are written and esteem them as things of naught" (2 Ne. 33:2).

Maybe that condition could be described as spiritual cholesterol! If the heart is not hardened, then the Spirit can enter. The Spirit presents its message and witness unto the heart. Each of us determines whether it also enters into the heart. For those who receive it, there is a power from on high that creates a spiritual strength within their souls. Concerning that enabling power I would like to share a very meaningful experience.

A number of years ago, I received an early-morning telephone call from a young man with whom I had been privileged to share the teachings of the gospel. We had set an appointment for his baptism later that day, but he voiced a major concern. He said he hadn't slept that night because of his anxiety about the weightiness of his commitment to keep the covenants he would be making in connection with his baptism. He wanted to be faithful and obedient, but knew he also had weaknesses. He didn't want to make promises he wondered if he had strength to keep. He did not want to be a hypocrite by making a promise and then breaking it.

I praised him for his sincere concerns and integrity. I also agreed with him about his inability to keep his covenants in his current situation. But then I told him he would not be alone in his efforts to live in accordance with the Lord's expectations. So far he had received a witness of the Spirit to know the gospel was true. The Spirit had also created a desire within him to do what he should. He needed to have the faith that receiving the gift of the Holy Ghost would empower him with sufficient strength to be faithful as long as he allowed it to enter and remain within his heart. By the power of the Holy Ghost he would have the capacity to keep all the covenants he would ever make.

I assured him that when he received the gift of the Holy Ghost, he would have access to a spiritual power beyond his own strength, and that power would enable him to do whatever the Lord required of him. His capacity to be faithful and obedient would be enlarged. He would just have to trust the Lord to keep His promises and proceed to do what he knew he should. Along with my words of testimony came the confirmation of the Spirit, and peace replaced the pressure of opposing persuasions. The young man was baptized and, as a recipient of the power of the Spirit, has continued his pursuit of happiness along the road to eternal life.

Those who have access to this Spirit, the gift of such great worth, must not view unwholesome movies or magazines or listen to degrading talk or music. No one can participate in unwholesome or unworthy practices *without losing* the Spirit, and thus be deprived of the capacity to see through and rise above the pernicious and alluring ways of the devil.

Those who say it does not matter if they hear or see unclean things need to be reminded that the accompanying loss of the power of the Spirit is a serious matter. We refer to an incident in the lives of the Nephites following the Savior's resurrection. The people were gathered around the temple and were conversing about Jesus Christ. Following that conversation, we read:

And it came to pass that while they were thus conversing one with another, they heard a voice as if it came out of heaven; and they cast their eyes round about, for they understood not the voice which they heard; and it was not a harsh voice, neither was it a loud voice; nevertheless, and notwithstanding it being a small voice it did pierce them that did hear to the center, insomuch that there was no part of their frame that it did not cause to quake; yea, it did pierce them to the very soul, and did cause their hearts to burn (3 Ne. 11:3).

I wonder if that voice would have spoken or if that voice would have been heard had they been conversing about something less spiritual, something that would degrade the mind—something that would cause them to lose the capacity to receive communication from heavenly voices. They were conversing about Jesus Christ and were in such a state of mind that they could hear.

For most of us, the voice we hear from heaven is not an audible voice, not one that we might consciously record or describe, but it is a real voice. It is the voice of the Spirit. It is a voice that pierces the soul and causes hearts to burn. It is a voice of truth, desire, and power. It is the voice of the Spirit. How much is it worth to know what is right? How much is it worth to desire to do what is right? How much is it worth to have the capacity to do what is right? When we rely on the power of the Spirit, we go forth with the capability of discerning, desiring, and doing. As always, we look to the Savior for a pattern. Of Him, the Prophet Joseph Smith said, "None ever were perfect but Jesus; and why was He perfect? Because He was the Son of God, and *had the fullness of the Spirit, and greater power* than any man" (*TPJS*, 187–88; emphasis added). (See also *Joseph Smith Translation*, John 3:34.)

We know Jesus was perfect, and we may assume that He was perfect because He was God's Son. It is true—He was and is. But that isn't the reason He was perfect. There had to be more. The clue is contained in the statement above. He had the fullness of the Spirit, a source of His great power. But He was not born with the power of the Spirit. Rather He came without even a remembrance of His premortal identity and experience as a creator God. Elder James E. Talmage has written: "Over His mind had fallen the veil of forgetfulness common to all who are born to earth, by which the remembrance of primeval existence is shut off. The Child grew, and with growth there came to Him expansion of mind, development of faculties, and progression in power and understanding. His advancement was from one grace to another" (*Jesus the Christ,* 111–12). (See also D&C 93:11–13.)

After entering mortality, Jesus grew and developed in spiritual power until He had a fullness of the power of the Spirit enabling Him to meet and resist all forms of temptation and to rise above all kinds of pain and afflictions. (See Alma 7:11.)

The pattern is clear. We too can have power to overcome things we confront, so long as we continue to provide an environment for the Spirit to be comfortable within us. As we pay the price of worthiness, we truly perceive the Spirit to be a gift of great worth and the means of obtaining power from on high.

CHAPTER 9
THE POWER OF THE MIGHTY CHANGE

In a stake conference, the General Authority visitor counseled members to be more than "cosmetic Mormons." He suggested that membership in the Church must mean much more than church attendance. Perhaps that is what Elder Spencer W. Kimball had in mind when he declared, "There are many people in this Church today who think they live, but they are dead to the spiritual things. And I believe even many who are making pretenses of being active are also spiritually dead. Their service is much of the letter and *less of the spirit*" (CR, Apr. 1951, 103–06; emphasis added).

President Ezra Taft Benson has reminded us of the Lord's definition of Church membership: "Whosoever repenteth and cometh unto me, the same is my church" (D&C 10:67). President Benson then taught that an "important principle for us to understand if we would be true members of the Church is that repentance involves not just a change of actions, but a change of heart" ("A Mighty Change of Heart," *Ensign,* Oct. 1989, 2–5).

In this chapter we will illuminate the process by which the change of heart is accomplished and use as a primary text Alma's great discourse to the citizens of Zarahemla found in the fifth chapter of the book of Alma. Excluding the Savior's teachings, many consider Alma's sermon on the need for a change of heart as one of the greatest recorded in all holy writ. In his sermon, Alma provided a formula for the process of change as well as critical inquiries for a person to evaluate his current spiritual condition. Following Alma's preaching tour among his people, he later concluded that "the *preaching of the word* had a great tendency to lead the people to do that which was just—yea, it had had more powerful effect upon the minds of the people than the sword, or anything else" (Alma 31:5; emphasis added).

The change involved is a process of obtaining the power of the gospel. Man has not the power to make the spiritual change that is required. Only through gaining access to power from on high is the change possible. This conversion from one state of being to another has been variously described by latter-day Apostles. Each of the following emphasizes the need for a change to take place.

For instance, Elder Bruce R. McConkie has written:

> In the full gospel sense, however, conversion is more—far more—than merely changing one's belief from that which is false to that which is true; it is more than the acceptance of the verity of gospel truths, [more] than the acquirement of a testimony. To convert is to change from one status to another, and gospel conversion consists in the transformation of man from his fallen and carnal state to a state of saintliness. A convert is one who . . . has been born again: where once he was spiritually dead, he has been regenerated to a state of spiritual life. . . . He changes his whole way of life, and the nature and structure of his very being is quickened and changed *by the power of the Holy Ghost* (*Mormon Doctrine,* 2nd ed., 162; emphasis added).

The conversion and transformation process was also described by Elder Mark E. Petersen as follows:

That birth of the spirit means something more than most of us normally realize. Through proper teaching, a conviction is born in our soul. Faith develops. Through it we see how important it is to become like Christ. We see ourselves as we are in contrast to a Christ-like soul. A desire for a change-over is born within us. The change-over begins. We call it repentance. Through our faith and as part of our conversion or change from one state to another, we begin to see sin in its true light. . . . We strive with all our souls to become like the Savior ("The Power of Testimony," Address to Seminary and Institute Faculty, Brigham Young University, July 11, 1956).

This spiritual change, or rebirth, is also addressed by President David O. McKay, who declared:

No man can sincerely resolve to apply in his daily life the teachings of Jesus of Nazareth without sensing a change in his own nature. The phrase "born again" has a deeper significance than many people attach to it. This changed feeling may be indescribable, but it is real. Happy the person who has truly sensed the uplifting, transforming power that comes from this nearness to the Savior, this kinship with the Living Christ (CR, Oct. 1963, 23–26).

And from Elder Marion G. Romney, we learn the following about the mighty change of heart:

As used in the scriptures, "converted" generally implies not merely mental acceptance of Jesus and his teachings but also a motivating faith in him and in his gospel—a faith which works a transformation, an actual change in one's understanding of life's meaning and in his allegiance to God—in interest, in thought, and in conduct. While conversion may be accomplished in stages, one is not really converted in the full sense of the term unless and until he is at heart a new person. "Born again" is the scriptural term (CR, Oct. 1963, 23–26).

In the century before the coming of Christ, Alma observed a spiritual deterioration among the Nephite members of the Church. The Book of Mormon records that they "began to wax proud"; there "began to be great contentions among the people of the church," the "wickedness of the church was a great stumbling-block," and "the church began to fail in its progress" (Alma 4:6, 9–10). The seriousness of this condition caused Alma such great concern that he gave up his office as chief judge over the Nephites to go among them ". . . to stir them up in remembrance of their duty, and that he might pull down, *by the word of God,* all the pride and craftiness and all the contentions which were among his people" (Alma 4:19; emphasis added).

Alma could see there was "no way that he might reclaim [his people] save it were in bearing down in pure testimony against them" (Alma 4:19). Knowing the need for the Church members to experience a change of heart, he delivered powerful sermons throughout the land, beginning with the people of Zarahemla. He was true to his original intent as he identified his teachings as the word of God with noticeable frequency throughout his discourses.

Using the techniques of a master teacher, Alma began his sermon by selecting familiar incidents from the past. He noted how the Lord had delivered his people from bondage on previous occasions, emphasizing that this freedom was not obtained through the wisdom or cunning of men, but rather came as the result of divine intervention and "by *the power* of his word" (Alma 5:5; emphasis added).

Alma then asked the Church members three questions (see Alma 5:6), each of which dealt with an increasingly important point of emphasis. First he asked if they recalled the captivity of their fathers. Next, he asked if they remembered that their deliverance was much more than just a deliverance from physical bondage—they had been in spiritual bondage, and the Lord had extended His mercy and long-suffering in their behalf. The real issue was that the Lord had provided them with a freedom from sin. Alma then intensified his point with a third question, asking if they realized that the Lord had actually provided His people with the deliverance of their souls from hell.

Each of the three questions contained the phrase, "Have you sufficiently retained in remembrance?" It was not a matter of having intellectual recall of historical events. The people may have been capable of rehearsing the factual details, but the question went further: "Have you sufficiently remembered?" Alma seems to have been asking if their awareness of information included an understanding of its application and value to them. His asking seems to imply that they had either missed the message or failed to apply its teachings in their own lives.

Scriptural usage of the word *remembrance* often suggests more than recall of memory. The Lord has directed us to "always remember him" (D&C 20:77), though He surely would not expect a constant mental focus on Him to the exclusion of all other subjects or thoughts. Rather, we should remember to never deviate from the teachings and influence of the Lord and His Spirit. Thus, our remembering Him would be manifest in our lives if we reflect the Lord's standards and teachings.

Alma's inquiries about a "sufficient remembrance" imply that *sufficient* means not only an adequate amount, but also a quality level of awareness of the Lord's blessings. Alma had undoubtedly learned the need for remembering from the angel who appeared to him while he was still mired in sin. He was told, "Go, and remember the captivity of thy fathers in the land of Helam, and in the land of Nephi; and remember how great things [the Lord] has done for them" (Mosiah 27:16). That message triggered a chain of events that resulted in a mighty change in Alma's soul. It is of little wonder that Alma often chose a similar method of instructing the Saints. (See Alma 9:9–10; 29:11.)

After emphasizing the need for the people to remember the events of the past, Alma declared that the Lord had changed the hearts of their forebears. He had awakened them from a deep spiritual sleep by the light of the word of God, which brought the power to make the change. Though they were unaware, they had been facing everlasting destruction because their real bondage was spiritual—caused by the binding power of the "chains of hell" (Alma 5:7).

And what are the chains of hell? To the rebellious Church members in Ammonihah, Alma warned of these chains in the following way: "And they that will harden their hearts, *to them is given the lesser portion of the word until they know nothing concerning his mysteries;* and then they are taken captive by the devil, and led by his will down to destruction. Now this is what is meant by the chains of hell" (Alma 12:11; emphasis added).

From his prison in Liberty, Missouri, the Prophet Joseph Smith wrote of the satanic spirit that had "so strongly riveted the creeds of the fathers, who have inherited lies, upon the hearts of the children, and filled the world with confusion . . . and is now the very mainspring of all corruption" (D&C 123:7). He further referred to this satanic influence as "an iron yoke, . . . a strong band; . . . handcuffs, and chains, and shackles, and fetters of hell" (D&C 123:8). In other words, Satan substitutes false ideas to bind people in a state of spiritual bondage, which can only be resisted or overcome by an awareness and acceptance of the word of God.

Centuries before Alma's day, Lehi also pleaded with his sons to "awake from a deep sleep, yea, even from the sleep of hell, and shake off the awful chains by which ye are bound, which are the chains which bind the children of men, that they are carried away captive down to the eternal gulf of misery and woe" (2 Ne. 1:13).

He challenged them to awaken and "put on the armor of righteousness. Shake off the chains with which ye are bound" (2 Ne. 1:23). From a latter-day revelation we note that the "armor of righteousness" that would release them from the chains of hell includes the sword of the Lord, which is His word (see D&C 33:1).

Where do we find this valuable piece of armor, this word of the Lord? Though the Lord is the ultimate source of all truth, He uses at least three means to make the word of truth available to us, all of which come to us by means of power from on high. The word may come to us through (1) scriptural records, (2) the teachings of living prophets, and (3) the inspiration of the Holy Ghost, or any combination of these three. Jacob declared, "We search the prophets [scripture], and we have many revelations [living prophets] and the spirit of prophecy [testimony of Jesus provided by the Holy Ghost]" (Jacob 4:6; see also D&C 52:9, 36). We are not only instructed in the ways of the Lord, but we are also protected from being deceived by having an understanding of absolute truth. Any opinion or philosophical declaration that is out of harmony with the word of God is unacceptable and should be discarded in favor of the truth. Thus, the word of the Lord is a sword, a weapon of righteousness that cuts through the spiritually binding powers of the chains of hell.

Those who lay hold on the word of truth and trace it to its original source come to Christ (see Moro. 7:19). Gospel truths are as the spokes of a wheel, all emanating from Christ, who is the hub. Anyone who would accept and lay hold on these truths is consequently led to their author, Jesus Christ. This experience is depicted in Lehi's dream as holding on to the iron rod, or word of Christ, which leads people to Him. In reality, people are led to partake of the fruit of Christ—the fruit of the tree (see Alma 5:34)—which is the redeeming power of His Atonement. Thus, the center, the hub of life, should not be Christ alone but also what He did for us. Thus, when we come unto Christ, we are also preparing ourselves to partake of His Atonement, and thus our hearts are changed as certainly as was Lehi's.

Alma finished his historical review of the spiritual transformation of the fathers by declaring that the chains of hell were loosed from them and they were saved.

Still speaking in the context of that experience, Alma asked his congregation to consider the basis upon which salvation had been promised. He asked, "What grounds had they to hope for salvation? What is the cause of their being loosed from the bands of death, yea, and also the chains of hell?" (Alma 5:10). Answering his own questions, Alma then noted four conditions that had existed for them to obtain a hope for salvation (see Alma 5:11–13).

1. Follow the living prophet. They had to believe in the words of the prophet Abinadi when he spoke "the words of God" (Alma 5:11). They also had to follow the prophet Alma as he taught and led them through their periods of bondage. They did so with patience and faith (see Mosiah 23:21; 24:16). Consistently, the

Church in our own dispensation has been commanded to "give heed unto all [the prophet's] words and commandments . . . as if from mine own mouth, in all patience and faith" (D&C 21:4–5).

Why are patience and faith needed? Sometimes the prophet teaches or counsels on subjects or in ways not acceptable to some people. They may not see the reason to follow his instructions, but the Lord said to have patience, for in time the reason for such obedience will be manifest to all. In the meantime, the people have been commanded to have enough faith to act according to heavenly counsel based on the vision and understanding of a prophet and seer. If people wait to act until they see the reason, they may wait too long. To those who faithfully follow the Lord's living prophet comes the promise that "the gates of hell shall not prevail" (D&C 21:6). As an aside, we remember that the entire Book of Mormon scenario began with the story of Lehi listening to and following the counsel of living prophets (see 1 Ne. 1:4).

2. Have a mighty change wrought in the heart. Throughout the scriptures, the heart is mentioned symbolically as the repository of feelings. After his masterful and inspired sermon, King Benjamin asked his people if they believed the words he had spoken. Their unanimous response was, "Yea, we believe all the words which thou hast spoken unto us; and also, we know of their surety and truth, because of *the Spirit* of the Lord Omnipotent, which *has wrought a mighty change in us,* or in our hearts, that we have no more disposition to do evil, but to do good continually" (Mosiah 5:2). They continued by saying, "And we are willing to enter into a covenant with our God to do his will, and to be obedient to his commandments in all things" (Mosiah 5:5; emphasis added).

Any previous inclination to sin or be unfaithful to covenants had been replaced with the change of their very nature. Their feelings or desires had been changed as they had partaken of the fruit of the Atonement. People who are changed internally manifest that transition through a change in behavior externally. What we are determines what we do. Outward motions are predicated upon inward emotions or feelings.

We cannot bring about such a change in ourselves or others. It comes only from an internal conversion through the workings of the Spirit of the Lord. President Benson has said, "The Lord works from the inside out. The world works from outside in. The world would take people out of the slums. Christ takes the slums out of people, and then they take themselves out of the slums. The world would mold men by changing their environment. Christ changes men, who then change their environment. The world would shape human behavior, but Christ can change human nature" (CR, Oct. 1985, 4–6).

King Benjamin was pleased with the response of his people and identified the source and nature of the change as follows: "And now, because of the covenant which ye have made ye shall be called the children of Christ, his sons, and his daughters; for behold, this day he hath spiritually begotten you; for ye say that your hearts are changed through faith on his name; therefore, ye are born of him and have become his sons and his daughters" (Mosiah 5:7).

This spiritual rebirth is actually a third birth. Our first birth took place in the premortal world where all were born as spirit children of heavenly parents. We were called the sons and daughters of God, and spoke to and of him as our Father. Next, we came into mortality. All of us were born as physical children of earthly parents and subsequently forgot our previous residence, associations, and parentage. We received the name of our earthly father and learned to speak to and of him as our father. Finally, being born again or experiencing a spiritual rebirth is, first of all, to receive the redeeming powers of the Atonement, to be cleansed in the spirit, and to become innocent again, as we were at the time of our first and second births. (See D&C 93:38.) Thus, this rebirth provides the sanctification and cleansing that comes by the spirit and power of the Holy Ghost. We also become eventual heirs of another physical body in the Resurrection. Therefore, we take the name of Christ in this rebirth experience, since He is the father of both of these processes. Rightfully then, we are called the sons and daughters of Christ. When Alma experienced his own spiritual rebirth, he learned from the Lord that the requirement for spiritual rebirth pertains to all mortals: "Marvel not that all mankind, yea, men and women, all nations, kindreds, tongues and people, *must be born again;* yea, born of God, changed from their carnal and fallen state, to a state of righteousness, being redeemed of God, becoming his sons and daughters;

"And thus they become new creatures; and unless they do this, they can in nowise inherit the kingdom of God" (Mosiah 27:25–26; emphasis added).

Such a spiritual, internal transformation is truly described as a "mighty change." The phrase itself might suggest to some that they should have some form of dramatic experience. And well it may be, as in the case of Alma (see Alma 36:10–22). But for most, the process will likely be gradual and take place over a longer period of time, and will not be noticeable at any one point (see 3 Ne. 9:20). President Benson taught that this change "is a step by step, steady and consistent movement toward godliness" (*The Teachings of Ezra Taft Benson,* 71).

3. Trust in the true and living God. A trust in God is one of the fruits of faith. Unless we have an awareness of and confidence in God's knowledge and power, we will not adhere to or obey His laws and commandments. Without faith in an unseen yet living Lord, we mortals lack sufficient reason to act in accordance with His revealed law. This is especially true when divine directives cause discomfort or inconvenience, or require sacrifice.

Who would go through the uncomfortable process of repentance without a love for God and a conviction that following the Savior's way is essential to happiness and salvation? Would many of us give of our time and resources in providing service in the kingdom without the spiritual assurance that such effort extends hope to us and blesses others? How many would perform temple ordinances without personal evidence that the work done in those holy houses is eternal? Trust in God is essential before anyone can hope for salvation.

Perhaps the condition opposite to trusting in the Lord is setting our hearts upon the things of the world. Such things can be seen as the means of providing immediate satisfaction and reward for temporal labor. Alma warned against following this philosophy in a sermon he preached to the citizens of Gideon, when he said, ". . . I trust that ye have not set your hearts upon riches and the vain things of the world; yea, I trust that you do not worship idols, but that ye do worship the true and the living God, and that ye look forward for the remission of your sins, with an everlasting faith, which is to come" (Alma 7:6).

Placing our trust in worldly things rather than in a living God is idolatry. President Spencer W. Kimball identified the practice of idolatry as "among the most serious of sins" and described its object as "anything which is earthly in any form. It would include both tangible and less tangible things, and everything which entices a person away from duty, loyalty, and love for and service to God" (*Miracle of Forgiveness*, 40).

4. Endure to the end. In our dispensation, the Lord declared, "He only is saved who endureth unto the end" (D&C 53:7). It is not enough to forsake the world by coming unto Christ in the covenant-making process of baptism. We must continue in the struggle to overcome the world by keeping the conditions of that covenant. Yielding to the enticings of Satan at any time after coming unto Christ takes personal purity and spiritual power away from us. Even though we may live a significant portion of our lives in righteousness, we are powerless to prevent subsequent sin from destroying the fruits of previous spiritual living. King Benjamin taught his people that they had to obtain a forgiveness for sin and retain it as well:

> As ye have come to the knowledge of the glory of God, or if ye have known of his goodness and have tasted of his love, and have received a remission of your sins, which causeth such exceedingly great joy in your souls, even so I would that ye should remember, and always retain in remembrance, the greatness of God, . . . and humble yourselves even in the depths of humility, calling on the name of the Lord daily, and standing steadfastly in the faith of that which is to come, . . .
>
> And behold, I say unto you that if ye do this ye shall always rejoice, and be filled with the love of God, and always retain a remission of your sins (Mosiah 4:11–12).

Giving way to subsequent sin brings the return of former sins and their consequences (see D&C 82:7). Being steadfast in righteousness is an ongoing requirement of all who hope for salvation. Elder Bruce R. McConkie declared, "All the faithful Saints, all of those who have endured to the end, depart this life with the absolute guarantee of eternal life" (CR, Oct. 1976, 158).

After summarizing the conditions upon which the fathers had obtained their hope for salvation, Alma put the value of knowledge gleaned from the past into true perspective, giving it a personal and present application. History not applied is of little value.

Alma asked his listeners, "And now behold, I ask of you, my brethren of the church, have ye spiritually been born of God? Have ye received his image in your countenances? Have ye experienced this mighty change in your hearts?" (Alma 5:14).

Knowing how others attained a hope for salvation is useful only when we follow that same eternal pattern and experience for ourselves the spiritual rebirth and the mighty change of heart.

I once discussed with my wife what Alma might have meant when he referred twice to having God's image in our countenances. (See Alma 5:14, 19.) I asked her specifically, "What is God's image?" Her answer was, "It is a reflection of perfection." I thought that was a great answer. Many people assume that attaining perfection is reserved for some future life and certainly is not possible to attain in this one. Yet the Savior commanded mortals to become perfect. President Kimball explained that "being perfect means to triumph over sin. This is a mandate from the Lord. He is just and wise and kind. He would never require anything from his children which was not for their benefit and which was not attainable. Perfection therefore is an achievable goal" (*Miracle of Forgiveness,* 209). Moroni closed the Book of Mormon record with this challenge:

> Yea, come unto Christ, and be perfected in him, and deny
> yourselves of all ungodliness; and if ye shall deny yourselves
> of all ungodliness, and love God with all your might, mind
> and strength, then is his grace sufficient for you, that by his
> grace ye may be perfect in Christ; and if by the grace of

God ye are perfect in Christ, ye can in nowise deny the power of God.

And again, if ye by the grace of God are perfect in Christ, and deny not his power, then are ye sanctified in Christ by the grace of God, through the shedding of the blood of Christ, which is in the covenant of the Father unto the remission of your sins, that ye become holy, without spot (Moro. 10:32–33).

We may lack many qualities of perfection, yet through Christ we can be as free from sin as He is. We can be perfect in this manner in this life through repentance. We can have the image of God in our countenances now.

Alma continued his teaching with questions. They might serve as a checklist that determines if we really do have God's image in our countenances. He asked the Church members to look forward to the time of their judgment, when everyone will stand before the Lord in one of three conditions:

1. **The blessed.** These individuals have repented and have been faithful to the conditions of salvation. Their "works have been the works of righteousness upon the face of the earth" (Alma 5:16).

2. **The liars.** These people are unrepentant, but think they can lie and misrepresent their works as having been righteous. They think such prevarication can obtain for them a hope of salvation (see Alma 5:17).

3. **The guilty.** These people are also unrepentant, but they make no pretense through misrepresentation. They will find their souls "filled with guilt and remorse, having a . . . perfect remembrance of all [their] wickedness, yea,

a remembrance that [they] have set at defiance the commandments of God" (Alma 5:18). Such persons cannot hope for salvation.

As if to summarize what he had taught, Alma asked the all-encompassing question: "I say unto you, can ye look up [to God] at that day with a pure heart and clean hands?" (Alma 5:19). His question is a reminder that our souls are both physical and spiritual (see D&C 88:15), and that both need to be free from sin. David of old posed a similar question when he asked, "Who shall ascend into the hill of the Lord? or who shall stand in his holy place?" The answer? "He that hath clean hands, and a pure heart; who hath not lifted up his soul unto vanity, nor sworn deceitfully" (Ps. 24:3–4).

We are all responsible for controlling our physical bodies and behaving in accordance with standards of righteousness. In the waters of baptism, we establish covenants that conform to the example of Jesus Christ and His baptismal commitments. "But notwithstanding he being holy, he showeth unto the children of men that, according to the flesh he humbleth himself before the Father, and witnesseth unto the Father that he would be obedient unto him in keeping his commandments" (2 Ne. 31:7). He promised to make His flesh be obedient; keep His hands clean and maintain an unblemished soul; be pure in heart. His baptismal commitment "showeth unto the children of men the straitness of the path, and the narrowness of the gate, by which they should enter, he having set the example before them" (2 Ne. 31:9).

In almost unbelievable contrast, some think and express the idea that they are powerless to control the innate desires of their flesh. Some are heard to say, "The Lord made me this way and I cannot help myself." Somehow, this rationalization is supposed to justify their yielding to fits of anger or succumbing to lusts of the flesh.

Another contrast is provided by those who feel that they have been thrust into an evil world of sinful influences and thus cannot be expected to rise above their environment. But the Lord's injunction to Adam and Eve has never been repealed. "I, God, blessed them, and said unto them: Be fruitful, and multiply, and replenish the earth, and subdue it, and have dominion" (Moses 2:28). The Lord expects all of us to subdue our environment and control its effect upon our souls. Lehi taught that the Messiah would "redeem the children of men from the fall. And because that they are redeemed from the fall they have become free forever, knowing good from evil; to act for themselves and not to be acted upon" (2 Ne. 2:26). We are to act; we are responsible for our actions. Covenant people are to subdue their flesh and thus have "clean hands."

Clean hands are an external reflection of pure thoughts and internal conditions that are symbolized by the phrase "pure of heart." No act was ever performed that did not originate as a thought in the mind. If we control our minds, we will also then control our bodies. What we do is predicated upon what we think and what we are. Our influence upon others is dependent upon our internal makeup. President David O. McKay said: "Every man and every person who lives in this world wields an influence, whether for good or for evil. It is not what he says alone; it is not alone what he does. It is what he is. Every man, every person radiates what he or she really is" (*The Instructor,* Oct. 1964, 373–74).

People with clean hands and pure hearts are those who have the "image of God engraven upon [their] countenances" (Alma 5:19).

Alma's next inquiry was directed to those who may have previously experienced the mighty change of conversion, but subsequently may have lost that powerful influence. He asked, "And now behold, I say unto you, my brethren, if ye have experienced a change of heart, and if ye have felt to sing the song of redeeming love, I would ask, can ye feel so now?" (Alma 5:26). It is not enough to experience the gospel once. There needs to be an ongoing, continual nurturing of the spirit, or the inner feelings that were once so predominant will dissolve. There must be a feeding of the spirit in order to have feelings of the Spirit.

Perhaps to provide a verification of worthiness, or to take inventory of current spiritual conditions, Alma asked some specific, searching questions of his listeners. First, he asked about maintaining a state of blamelessness before God. In other words, have old habits crept back, or have previously uncontrolled thoughts reestablished themselves and created inappropriate behavior? If so, our hands would not still be clean and our hearts would no longer be pure.

Next, he asked about humility and wondered if they had been stripped of pride. C. S. Lewis observed that "as long as you are proud, you cannot know God. A proud man is always looking down on things and people; and, of course, as long as you are looking down, you cannot see something that is above you" (*Mere Christianity,* 96).

President Benson said: "Pride does not look up to God and care about what is right. It looks sideways to man and argues who is right. Pride is characterized by 'What do I want out of life?' rather than by 'What would God have me do with my life?' It is self-will as opposed to God's will. Humility responds to God's will—to the fear of His judgments and the needs of those around us. To the proud, the applause of the world rings in their ears; to the humble, the applause of heaven warms their hearts" (CR, Apr. 1986, 2–6).

Pride is a stumbling block in the path of Christ's followers. As Alma said, "Such an one hath not eternal life" (Alma 5:28).

Alma then asked about envy, which is mostly associated with worldly things. To set our minds on worldly things preempts having them on spiritual things. David Whitmer was chastised and Emma Smith was counseled on that subject (see D&C 30:2; 25:10). Worldly things cannot cleanse or save the soul. A mind saturated with or focused on worldliness denies access to the Spirit from on high and needs to be refocused.

Finally, Alma inquired about those who mock their brother or persecute him. As Brigham Young University professor Dr. Gary L. Bunker wrote:

> To mock is to humiliate, ridicule, insult, revile, make fun of, deride, sneer at, scorn, or hold in contempt. Occasions for mockery usually occur in the context of real or imagined differences. Differences in beliefs, wealth, learning, social position, physical characteristics, group membership, and behavior may be used as pretexts for the justification of mockery. Mockery costs our brother or sister severe physical and/or psychological pain. It also jeopardizes our hope of eternal life. Moreover, it is especially debilitating to those who have been called to serve. We cannot serve those for whom we have contempt ("Mocking Our Brother," *Ensign*, Apr. 1975, 36–41).

Just before Alma reminded his listeners that he was speaking to church members by way of commandment and to non-church members by way of invitation (see Alma 5:62), he provided another insight. In addition to his battery of deeply personal and spiritually searching questions, Alma asked one more significant question: "And now my beloved brethren, I say unto you, can ye withstand these sayings?" (Alma 5:53). To withstand them now is to likely stand without them forever. A mighty change is needed.

President Benson shared considerable insightful information along with a stimulating challenge to change:

> Can human hearts be changed? Why, of course! It happens every day in the great missionary work of the Church. It is one of the most widespread of Christ's modern miracles. If it hasn't happened to you—it should. Besides the physical ordinance of baptism and the laying on of hands, one must be spiritually born again to gain exaltation and eternal life. . . . Men changed for Christ will be captained by Christ. Like Paul they will be asking, "Lord, what wilt thou have me to do?" (Acts 9:6). Finally, men captained by Christ will be consumed in Christ. Their will is swallowed up in his will. (See John 5:30.) They do always those things that please the Lord. (See John 8:29.) Not only would they die for the Lord, but more important they want to live for Him. . . . May we be convinced that Jesus is the Christ, choose to follow Him, be changed for Him, captained by Him, consumed in Him, and born again (CR, Oct. 1985, 4–6).

We have spoken of a mighty change that occurred in our forebears, but the problems we face are now. We, too, need to have changed and pure hearts and place clean hands in contact with iron rods of gospel truths.

The mighty change is the result of the process that starts with hearing the word of God. Parents and priesthood and auxiliary leaders need to see to it that the word of the Lord is taught in and to families, members, and nonmembers. Otherwise, those without the gospel have no chance of experiencing the spiritual rebirth.

They will not have the power of God in their souls. They may be baptized and active, yet not be born again or receptive to spiritual power from on high. External motions may not reflect internal spiritual emotions.

We all must experience this mighty change of heart if we are to be more than "cosmetic Mormons." Our very countenances should reflect the image and perfection of God from an internalized spiritual rebirth. We must be spiritually alive here before we can hope to have salvation and eternal life hereafter.

No one really appreciates the magnitude of the mighty change unless and until he or she has experienced it. It is not just a principle of the gospel; it needs to be an experience with the gospel, and each of us can have it. There is a spiritual power associated with it. The power within is real, it comes from on high, and it changes hearts and lives.

CHAPTER 10
THE POWER TO STAND IN HOLY PLACES

With a seemingly increasing frequency, recent years have been filled with one disaster after another, some natural and some man-made. With some regularity there have been terrible earthquakes causing heavy death tolls and widespread destruction. We remember the mammoth tsunami in the Indian Ocean on December 26, 2004, that caused such a terrific loss of life. There have been tornados, tropical storms, and hurricanes that have taken loved ones and caused many people to be left homeless—without jobs, possessions, or security—and have left many without hope.

Our country, so long a sanctuary from invasion by foreign powers, has been the target of terrorists (on days like September 11, 2001) who have no respect for human life or property. As a result, our country has been thrust into wars in foreign lands and into a constant consciousness of the need for security at home. There are also acts of domestic violence reported in nearly every media newscast describing multitudinous incidents where our own citizens suffer at the hands of other human beings.

These conditions in our society and our world do not come as a surprise to us. The Lord has provided prophetic insights to us that are accurate descriptions of the destructive and debilitating activities awaiting the world, many of which presently surround us. We think of a few scriptural passages:

Plagues and destructions—D&C 29:15–21

Storms, earthquakes, and pestilences—D&C 43:21–25

Wars, iniquity, scourge, and desolations—D&C 45:26–33

Wars and fear—D&C 63:33

Wars, famine, and plague—D&C 87:1–2, 6

Tempests and seas beyond their bounds—D&C 88:88–91

Even more serious than these physically destructive forces are the spiritually decimating fruits sown in temptation, of which so many people partake. The Apostle Paul referred to the conditions of our day as "perilous times" (see 2 Tim. 3:1). Clearly, we face perils of entrapment by insidious snares of sin that are far more harmful to us and our spiritual well-being than any physical afflictions we might encounter.

So with all the turmoil, what should we do to be safe, and how can we help provide safety for loved ones and others with whom we have association? The Lord answers the question by telling us to "stand in holy places" (see D&C 45:32; 87:8; 101:22). Where is a holy place? People often think of temples, churches and homes. All of these qualify. However, we spend a great amount of time in places other than those mentioned, so there must be a broader definition.

The third personage in the Godhead is a spirit personage who bears the title of *Holy* Spirit or *Holy* Ghost because He is holy—or, in other words, He is free from sin. There are no sin-caused blemishes in His being and no restrictions or limitations to His having a fulness of spiritual power. So *wherever* and with *whomever* the Holy Spirit abides, that place or person is holy, being filled with some measure of spiritual power, which could ultimately become "a fulness of the Holy Ghost" (D&C 109:15).

Every Latter-day Saint is a recipient of the gift of the Holy Ghost, thereby having claim upon the presence of the Holy Spirit along with its attendant gifts. (For a description of many of these gifts, see D&C, 46:8–33; and Moro. 10:5–19.) Quite obviously, the person must also be holy in order to merit the fulness of spiritual power. That level of worthiness is attained by being free from sin, which everyone can be. We need to keep the commandments, or if we slip into sinful behavior we need to repent, obtain forgiveness through the Savior's Atonement, and be cleansed or sanctified by the Holy Spirit (see Alma 13:12). Thus, we are holy and qualify for an outpouring of spiritual powers. The Lord declared that the gifts of the spirit ". . . are given for the benefit of those who love me and keep all my commandments, *and him that seeketh so to do*" (D&C 46:9; emphasis added).

The name *saint* by which we are known means "holy." (See James E. Talmage, *The Latter-day Prophets and The Doctrine and Covenants*, 4:160.) So when we are worthy of that name, we are literally "latter-day holy ones," enjoying the presence of the Holy Spirit and the spiritual power He provides. Wherever there is a presence of the Holy Spirit, that place is holy, though it may not be a temple or church. When we are worthy of the Spirit, we are always standing in holy places, *wherever we may be.* By so doing, we are spiritually safe from all satanic-inspired temptations. If we should be a target of evil designs of wicked people or in the path of natural disasters, the Lord's Spirit will warn us. By being spiritually receptive, we have opportunity to escape from harm.

In a discourse on the Holy Ghost, the Savior said, "When he, the Spirit of truth [Holy Ghost], is come, he will guide you into all truth . . . and *he will shew you things to come*" (John 16:13; emphasis added). To those in our dispensation who serve the Lord in righteousness, He said, "To them will I reveal all mysteries . . . even the wonders of eternity shall they know, and *things to come will I show them* . . . For by my Spirit will I enlighten them" (D&C 76:7–8, 10; emphasis added).

Elder Marion G. Romney counseled: "Now, my brothers and sisters, we need to seek that Spirit. We need to realize that it is a real guide. Now, I tell you that you can make every decision in your life correctly if you can learn to follow the guidance of the Holy Spirit. This you can do if you will discipline yourself to yield your own feelings to the promptings of the Spirit" (CR, Oct. 1961, 60–61).

The way has been provided whereby we can be physically and spiritually safe in these troubled times. The Lord has promised His power, and He keeps His promises.

After the prophet Alma both blessed and cursed this promised land (depending on the righteousness or wickedness of the inhabitants), he pronounced another blessing upon eligible church members, describing and qualifying them by an interesting phrase: "And now, when Alma had said these words he blessed the church, yea, all those who should stand fast in the faith from that time henceforth" (Alma 45:17).

"Stand fast in the faith" is a figure of speech with symbolic meaning. First, let's clarify what it does *not* mean. "Stand" has no more relevance to a physical position of posture than "fast" refers to relative speed. For instance, everyone knows a flag does not have the means to *stand* independent of means of support. Yet when we Americans pledge allegiance to it we mention that it stands for our republic of the United States of America. The flag is a constant representation of the country and its capacity to provide liberty and justice for all. Likewise, righteous Saints are constant representatives of the Savior, whose name they bear. Sacramental prayers are reminders that they are not only willing, but that they do always remember the Savior and keep His commandments (see D&C 20:77, 79).

So what does it mean for Church members to stand *fast*? The term implies a similar unwavering firmness and permanence.

Those who stand fast are not people who fluctuate on matters of standards, doctrine, or commitment. Rather they are firmly planted pillars of power. People who are too weak in their faith to face and overcome satanic-inspired opposition lose their capacity to stand fast and, if not corrected, forfeit their spiritual inheritance hereafter. We seek to be among those who possess the strength to defy the hordes of evildoers who, with their deceptively evil ways, seek to entrap and conquer the unaware and unsuspecting youth and members of the Church. President Boyd K. Packer referred to the works of faithful Saints across the world and said, "We have felt the power in their simple faith. . . . Let no one underestimate the power of faith in the ordinary Latter-day Saints" ("Simple Faith," *Church News,* Oct. 9, 2004, 17).

We remember the giant Philistine named Goliath who stood in defiance of Israel's army and Israel's God. None of the soldiers of Israel dared to face him. But David, the shepherd boy, simply said, "Is there not a cause?" (1 Sam. 17:29). He then proceeded to use the resources available to him and, with faith in his God, ran directly at the representation of evil and destroyed it. The courage, strength, and faith of one young man earned the respect and changed the attitude of the entire army of Israel. In David's mind, the "cause" was sufficient reason to stand and not only face, but overcome, the seemingly overwhelming odds of the opposition. But David fought with more than his own strength. He had access to powers from on high, and he could not fail. He stood in a holy place.

When Jesus said that His disciples should stand in holy places, we remember that He defined a *disciple* as one who not only follows Him, but also receives His law and lives it (see D&C 41:5). Such a person is blessed with the ever-present companionship of the Holy Ghost and has the opportunity to bring holiness to the places he visits. Only true disciples of Jesus can do that. The

Prophet Joseph wrote an impassioned plea to the early brethren in the Church: "Brethren, shall we not go on in so great a cause? Go forward and not backward. Courage, brethren; and on, on to the victory!" (D&C 128:22).

In our own day, I vividly remember what happened one year at Fort Knox, Kentucky. A class of 110 newly commissioned Army officers had been undergoing training there through the winter months. More than 100 of them were on active duty only for the period of the training and would then revert to civilian status. They were away from home, and most of them felt they were away from any semblance of restriction from having a good time as they defined the term.

There were two members of The Church of Jesus Christ of Latter-day Saints in that class. There were only three in the class who refrained from participation in the drinking and carousing antics of the rest of the class. But only one of those nonparticipants was a Latter-day Saint. The other member of the Church felt he wanted to be accepted by the group and so compromised his Church standards and fell into the ways of the majority.

When spring graduation came around, a selection of class leaders was to be made for the final parade and other graduation exercises. Each one of the 110 officers was to assign a number to each of the other officers in the class, ranking them as to their character, integrity, and overall leadership skills. The results were astonishing. This class, which consisted mostly of men who compromised many personal standards and values, made a most unusual determination. The top two men selected by them were two of the three who did not participate in the drinking and partying activities of the rest. However, the Church member who had joined them in those same activities was ranked in the bottom ten. He, who was under covenant to stand against evil, lost even the respect of those he joined.

There is an honor and virtue vested in those who have the strength and courage to stand fast in a righteous cause. Samuel Smiles wrote:

> The courage that displays itself in silent effort and endeavor— that dares to endure all and suffer all for truth and duty—is more truly heroic than the achievements of physical valor, which are rewarded by honors and titles, or by laurels sometimes steeped in blood.
>
> It is moral courage that characterizes the highest order of manhood and womanhood—the courage to seek and to speak the truth; the courage to be just; the courage to be honest; the courage to resist temptation; the courage to do one's duty. If men and women do not possess this virtue, they have no security whatever for the preservation of any other (quoted by Elder Vaughn J. Featherstone in *The Disciple of Christ*, 21).

I remember interviewing a young woman for her temple recommend just prior to her eternal marriage in the temple. I asked her if she was morally clean. I shall never forget her answer. She said, "Yes I am, and I always have been." Many can say that about certain other standards of the Church. Those who cannot say so now need greater strength than they had in the past. But if they seek and obtain that strength through the power of the Savior's Atonement and His mercy, they can eventually answer a similar question by saying, "Yes I am, and I always will be." Then they too will stand in holy places.

For those who have not acquired either the vision of values or the strength inherent in a vessel of cleanliness through whom the Holy Spirit flows, there is but one way to change their status. Some have mistakenly thought they could willfully sin and then conveniently confess to a priesthood leader in order to qualify for the magnificent blessings of priesthood ordinances and covenants bestowed upon the worthy in sacred temples. Some have even chosen to avoid seeking sacred covenants because of a perceived inconvenience to them, or for reasons of perceived unpopularity.

True repentance is not such a casual experience or process. There are those who have thought a brief or simple visit with the bishop would constitute sufficient repentance, and some have even thought they could deceive the bishop and thus avoid any painful or distasteful experience altogether. To all such misinformed persons, the prophet Jacob gave clear instruction concerning the need to plead with the Master for forgiveness of all sins. He said: "O then, my beloved brethren, come unto the Lord, the Holy One. Remember that his paths are righteous. Behold, the way for man is narrow, but it lieth in a straight course before him, and the keeper of the gate is the Holy One of Israel; and he employeth no servant there; and there is none other way save it be by the gate; for he cannot be deceived, for the Lord God is his name" (2 Ne. 9:41).

Elder Vaughn J. Featherstone emphasized the divine source of the great cause in which we presently labor, even that of seeking eternal exaltation, building the Lord's kingdom, and assisting Him in saving the souls of His children:

Imagine with me the magnitude of the cause in which we are engaged. We have been given the keys, the priesthood, and the program for the greatest cause in eternity. . . .

The cause is greater than men or prophets. It is the cause of the Savior. It is the cause of God the Eternal Father. By enlisting in His cause and faithfully enduring, we will be the recipients of all we are teaching and sharing.

. . . Imagine a cause with eternal implications and consequences, a cause so great that all eternity hangs in the balance as we accept or reject it. We do not fully comprehend what a magnificent privilege it is to be fully enlisted (*The Incomparable Christ*, 114–15).

So where does one get the strength to stand fast in holy places? Nephi answers: ". . . whoso would hearken unto the word of God, and would *hold fast* unto it, they would never perish; neither could the temptations and the fiery darts of the adversary overpower them unto blindness, to lead them away to destruction" (1 Ne. 15:24; emphasis added).

For a number of years, I was often assigned the responsibility of reorganizing stake presidencies and had the privilege of participating in the search for the man whom the Lord would have as the new stake president. After learning whom the Lord had chosen, the call was extended. It was common for the brother to express his feelings of inadequacy, but express his acceptance of the call and commit himself to do his best. That is an admirable promise. Doing one's best is obviously expected by the Lord and is certainly essential to the successful accomplishment of duty, but it is clearly not adequate by itself. That concept is imbedded in Nephi's statement that ". . . it is by grace that we are saved [or blessed or strengthened], after all we can do" (2 Ne. 25:23).

We turn to the following explanation of the term *grace:*

The main idea of the word is divine means of help or strength, given through the bounteous mercy and love of Jesus Christ. . . .

It is likewise through the grace of the Lord that individuals, through faith in the atonement of Jesus Christ and repentance of their sins, receive strength and assistance to do good works that they otherwise would not be able to maintain if left to their own means. *This grace is an enabling power* that allows men and women to lay hold on eternal life and exaltation after they have expended their own best efforts. . . .

Grace cannot suffice without total effort on the part of the recipient (Bible Dictionary, "Grace," 697; emphasis added).

Following are a few examples of the principle. When Nephi was asked to return to Jerusalem to obtain the brass plates, he knew it was a commandment from the Lord. He explained why he would go and how he knew he could accomplish the assigned task. He said, "The Lord giveth no commandments . . . save he shall prepare a way for them that they may accomplish the thing which he commandeth them" (1 Ne. 3:7).

Nephi and his brothers embarked upon a very difficult assignment. Twice they made effort, under the direction and leadership of the older brothers, to obtain the plates, and they failed both times. When Laman and Lemuel were about to return to their father in the wilderness (and probably report that they had done their best), Nephi declared with an oath that they would not go down until they had accomplished their assignment (see 1 Ne. 3:14–15).

Nephi subsequently "was led by the Spirit, not knowing beforehand the things which [he] should do" (1 Ne. 4:6). He was then successful in doing the Lord's bidding. Nephi may not have been any more imaginative, skilled, or intelligent than his brothers. All of them may very well have done their best; but it wasn't enough. Only Nephi accessed the Lord's power after all he could do and, of course, that was sufficient.

The brother of Jared faced the difficult problem of not having light in the barges. He asked the Lord for help, but the Lord responded to his inquiry by asking, "What will ye that I should do that ye may have light in your vessels?" (Ether 2:23). After the brother of Jared devised a plan and did the necessary work to implement it, the Lord willingly participated and provided the means of solving the problem.

Enoch felt inadequate, knowing his own limitations, and was certain he could not perform the task given him. But the Lord said unto him, "Anoint thine eyes with clay, and wash them, and thou shalt see. And he did so" (Moses 6:35). Does anyone think the clay had anything to do with his seeing? The Lord wants us to be involved. He allows us opportunity to stand fast in our faith, focus on solutions to problems, and expend effort before He does for us what we cannot do for ourselves.

Naaman was a Syrian captain, a man of valor, but he had leprosy. He went to the prophet Elijah for a healing blessing after hearing of his prophetic powers. But when Naaman arrived, Elijah sent a messenger to him and told him to dip in the Jordan River seven times. Naaman was angry about that, for he thought all that would be necessary was for him to meet the prophet, be healed of his disease, and go on his way. None of that happened. His friends convinced him that he should do as he was told, so he did. After dipping himself seven times, the leprosy was cleansed from his body. He needed to be involved and obey instructions. He needed to do what he could do before expecting the powers from on high to be extended in his behalf. Heavenly powers are not freely bestowed, though they are available.

I think of a young lady who was struggling with deep feelings of sorrow and regret for the serious sins she had allowed to come into her life. Among other things that were said, I felt impressed to tell her she should talk to her father about her situation. She vigorously resisted such an idea, saying that he would be very angry and upset with her for ignoring parental teachings and violating their trust. I suggested she should pray for strength and seek the Lord's help with the experience. Several days later, she returned to tell me she had talked with her father and wanted to share the story with me.

She said she was sitting on a couch and he in his favorite chair. Though she was nervous, she told him of the problems she had caused. He was silent for some time, and she became very frightened. Then, without saying a word, he arose and came to where she was seated, took hold of both her arms and lifted her to her feet. He then embraced her and said, "Oh, sweetheart, how have you carried such a heavy burden for so long without us?"

There is an element of fatherhood in that statement that goes beyond mortality. There is a Father in heaven who feels the same. Though He, like this young lady's father, could not come to her, He would respond when she came to Him. When we have done all we can do, then we can expect and obtain divine help. Sometimes we don't do the simple things we should and can do, things that may not appear to us to be important or essential. Washing one's eyes with clay, dipping in a river, avoiding the appearance or presence of evil—these are all simple acts. But they are things we can do, efforts we can make, a lifestyle we can live—all part of what we do when we are doing our best.

A young mother with small children had a wonderful marriage and life until her returned-missionary husband one day left her. But she still loved him. She had done nothing to destroy her feelings of love or break her marriage covenant; it was all still there. But her heart was broken. She cried a lot. One day she said she just couldn't stand it but didn't know what to do. When there was nothing she could do, something needed to be done for her.

Father Alma said to his son, "Whosoever shall put their trust in God shall be supported in their trials, and their troubles, and their afflictions, and shall be lifted up at the last day" (Alma 36:3). There was only one place for this young mother to find the support she needed. No one could soothe her heart or ease her pain but God, and He did. Sustaining power came from on high. Though the husband did not repent, the Lord comforted and supported her as she continued to live a productive and righteous life. The prophet Alma continued his counsel: "Cry unto God for all thy support; yea, let all thy doings be unto the Lord, and whithersoever thou goest let it be in the Lord; yea, let all thy thoughts be directed unto the Lord; yea, let the affections of thy heart be placed upon the Lord forever" (Alma 37:36).

When we have done our best, the Lord is there to make up the rest. A touring group of students from Brigham Young University were performing in Bulgaria. When I met this wonderful group of young people, I was asked by their leader if I could help one of the girls with a special problem she had encountered during the many days of their previous travels. I learned from her that something had gotten into her eye and caused serious vision impairment. Her sight was becoming dimmer each day, and she was almost blind in one eye. Adequate medical assistance had not been available where they had traveled, though they had sought for and received what could be provided by limited local resources. She asked if she could have a blessing. I looked into the eyes of this faithful, wonderful daughter of God and felt the presence of the Spirit. I felt the strength of her faith, and I knew Father had a blessing for her. She had done all she could do, but she could not repair her own eye. Father could, and He would, and He did.

Brigham Young spoke of the need for us individually to have access to spiritual powers:

Now those men, or those women, who know no more about *the power of God, and the influence of the Holy Spirit,* than to be led entirely by another person, suspending their own understanding, and pinning their fate upon another's sleeve, will never be capable of entering into the celestial glory. . . . They cannot rule themselves to say nothing of ruling others, but they must be dictated to in every trifle, like a child. They cannot control themselves in the least . . . somebody else must control them. They never can . . . be crowned as rulers with glory, immortality, and eternal lives. They never can hold scepters of glory, majesty, and power in the celestial kingdom. Who will? Those who are valiant and inspired with the true independence of heaven, who will go forth boldly in the service of their God, leaving others to do as they please, determined to do right, though all mankind . . . should take the opposite course. Will this apply to any of you? Your own hearts can answer (*JD,* 11:312, emphasis added).

We now conclude this chapter, as we began, with the reminder that each of us should determine to seek for and obtain sufficient strength and power to stand fast in our faith in Christ, His Atonement, and His gospel. Each of us should remember that when we do our best, the enabling power of His grace is sufficient for us to fulfill the Lord's expectations and our own righteous desires. We are then empowered with the presence of the Holy Spirit, and therefore will be found standing in holy places.

CHAPTER 11
THE POWER OF SACRIFICE

One of the first recorded commandments given to the first human beings, Adam and Eve, was that "they should worship the Lord their God, and should offer the firstlings of their flocks, for an offering unto the Lord" (Moses 5:5). It is apparent that the Lord considered sacrifice to be a part of the worship experience for His children. To better understand that connection, I will share a concept provided by Elder Russell M. Nelson of the Quorum of Twelve Apostles in a General Authority training meeting. He noted that the word *sacrifice* comes from two Latin roots. The first is *sacer*, meaning "sacred." The second is *facere*, meaning "to make." So the complete meaning of the word *sacrifice* is "to make sacred." Seeking to be in the spiritual presence of the Lord is a worship experience, made sacred by an appropriate offering of the worshiper. We see that sacrifice really has nothing to do with the commonly accepted notion that we give up something that belongs to us.

In this chapter we will discuss three of the categories in which we are to make sacrifice that contribute to a sacredness of our lives and our relationship with our Maker. First, we should hear the words of the Savior when He spoke from the heavens to the Nephites. Even before His appearance to them, He taught the people on this subject. He said: "And ye shall offer up unto me no more the shedding of blood; yea, your [blood] sacrifices and your burnt offerings shall be done away, for I will accept none of your [blood] sacrifices and your burnt offerings.

"And ye shall offer for a sacrifice unto me a broken heart and a contrite spirit" (3 Ne. 9:19–20).

This is the moment when the Savior announced the change in the law of sacrifice. Starting with Adam, the Lord's people obeyed the law of sacrifice for four thousand years by the shedding of blood; then He changed the form of observance. Christ's Atonement did away with blood sacrifice and changed the means whereby they should observe or keep the law. Instead of burnt offerings, the new way of complying with the law was to offer a broken heart and a contrite spirit. President J. Reuben Clark provided a most insightful commentary on that dramatic change of worship process:

> It is difficult for us today to realize the tremendous revolution involved in altering the ritualism of the Law of Moses into the humble and lowly concept of worship, not with the sacrificial blood of animals, but with this broken heart and contrite spirit of the worshiper. . . . But under the new covenant that came in with Christ, the sinner must offer the sacrifice out of his own life, not by offering the blood of some other creature; he must give up his sins, he must repent, he himself must make the sacrifice, and that sacrifice was calculated to reach out into the life of the sinner in the future so that he would become a better and changed man. This was a great evolutionary and revolutionary step in the development of righteousness among men (*Behold the Lamb of God,* 107–09).

Eighteen hundred years after the Lord spoke to the Nephites, He spoke on this subject again and reaffirmed the necessity of living the law of sacrifice in our dispensation. Once more He said, "Thou shalt offer a sacrifice unto the Lord thy God in righteousness, even that of a broken heart and a contrite spirit" (D&C 59:8; see also D&C 20:37). Two years later He inserted a very meaningful and interesting condition to the law. He said: "All among them who know their hearts are honest, and are broken, and their spirits contrite, *and are willing* to observe their covenants by sacrifice— yea, every sacrifice which I, the Lord, shall command—they are accepted of me" (D&C 97:8; emphasis added).

We note that our sacrifice experience must be a willing one. Otherwise, it is a hypocritical display that is certainly not a sacred offering; we are not drawn closer to the Lord through our pretense of worship, and we are not accepted of the Lord.

We will discuss three categories or different ways by which we observe the law of sacrifice:

1. Sacrifice of all earthly things

2. Giving away our sins

3. Denial of self

1. Sacrifice of All Earthly Things. This first requirement comes from a statement made by the Prophet Joseph Smith: "Let us here observe, that a religion that does not require the sacrifice of all things *never has power* [from on high] sufficient to produce the faith necessary unto life and salvation; for, from the first existence of man, the faith necessary unto the enjoyment of life and salvation never could be obtained without the sacrifice of all earthly things" (*Lectures on Faith,* 58, para. 7; emphasis added).

A willing sacrifice of all earthly things is prerequisite to obtaining the power from on high that interacts with and results from a faith in Christ unto salvation. If we want to increase our faith, we must acquire and develop a willingness to sacrifice all earthly things. If we are not willing, our faith will be in short supply. Earthly or worldly things can take many obvious forms, such as money, vehicles, houses, clothes, music, movies, books, etc. Other more subtle examples might include activities, styles, philosophies, time, interests, and attitudes. If and when any earthly thing comes between an individual and the Lord, a sacred relationship is damaged. The wise person willingly removes the obstacle and manifests sorrow and regret for allowing anything to interfere with a genuine and sincere worship experience with God. Only when one willingly sacrifices or removes the barrier that exists between him or her and the Lord does that person make sacred the relationship with the Lord. Then that person is in compliance with the law of sacrifice, is accepted of the Lord, and has access to spiritual powers.

One great example of a person sacrificing earthly things is a missionary. Everything just mentioned is part of a missionary's experience. Money that would have been earned by staying home and being employed—not to mention the money spent during the mission experience—is an earthly thing. The time given to the calling is earthly. Music, television, movies, cars, and stylish clothes are earthly things one does without. Athletics and personal interests are set aside. All of these things are discarded by missionaries that they might have greater faith and work more closely with the Holy Spirit in the Lord's work. Missionaries need spiritual power, and they acquire it as they remove barriers to their sacred and concentrated focus on the Lord. The First Presidency of the Church has guided and assisted missionaries to implement this principle by setting mission standards for them to follow.

I recall two young men who gave very different responses to mission calls and who had very different results in their lives. One told his bishop that he couldn't accept a call to serve because he had an athletic scholarship at a university and had a personal goal of going on to become a professional athlete. He felt a mission would drastically interfere with his goals. Unfortunately, his university experience did not turn out to be one in which he developed sufficient athletic skills to enter the professional ranks. He also drifted away from the Church while playing ball at the school.

The other young man had finished his undergraduate training in pre-medicine and had been accepted at a medical school where he could continue his studies and become a medical doctor, which was his long-standing hope for a professional career. But he accepted a call to serve a mission instead and notified the medical school that he would not be attending school after all. He did not know if he would have another opportunity for medical school two years later, but said he would still hope to do so. He would just wait and see when that time came.

He filled a wonderful mission, then returned to his former school for a year where he re-enrolled in classes he had already completed to refresh his mind in preparation for taking the medical exams again. He took them, did well, reapplied for a medical school appointment, and once more was accepted. He was heard to say that if he had not gotten into medical school he would still have no regrets for having filled a mission, because it was the greatest experience he could ever hope to have.

Many years ago, while serving in a stake presidency, I telephoned a young man who was a recently returned missionary. He had been home only a few days and was carrying a great spiritual power in his countenance. I said to him, "Elder, what are you doing tonight?" That was a terribly unfair question. I said it without thinking, but

I will never forget his answer. His response was immediate and spontaneous. He said, "Well, President, whatever it was, it is not nearly as important as whatever it is you have in mind. What would you like me to do tonight?"

In my mind I thanked God for such great youth. He did not take time to think about the question, and no one had to persuade him. He did not even have to know what I wanted. His priesthood leader was inquiring about the use of his time, and he willingly offered to give it. He was a young athlete who loved to play basketball, and I found out later that for the first time in two years he was going to play basketball with the ward team that night. But it didn't make any difference to him. I knew then what kind of missionary and Church member he was. I said to him, "Elder, I have a young lady in my office who would like to know more about the gospel. I thought maybe you would like to get a companion and come and teach her." He said he would love to, and he did. He would not let an earthly basketball game interfere.

President Marion G. Romney shared this story about himself:

About a quarter of a century ago Sister Romney and I moved into a ward in which they were just beginning to build a meetinghouse. The size of the contribution the bishop thought I ought to contribute rather staggered me. I thought it was at least twice as much as he should have asked. However, I had just been called to a rather high Church position, so I couldn't very well tell him where to go. Therefore, I said, "Well, I will pay it, Bishop, but I will have to pay it in installments because I don't have the money." And so I began to pay. And I paid and paid until I was down to about the last three payments, when, as is my habit, I was reading the Book of Mormon, and came to the scripture which said: "if a man . . . giveth a gift . . . grudgingly; wherefore it is counted unto him the same as if he had retained the gift; wherefore he is counted evil before God" (Moro. 7:8).

This shocked me because I was out about a thousand dollars. Well, I went on and paid the three installments I had promised to pay, and then I paid several more installments to convince the Lord that I had done it with the right attitude (*Relief Society Magazine,* Feb. 1968, 84–85).

Well might we imagine the conflict in President Romney's mind. He had gone through the entire process of making a sacrifice of earthly things, and it had not even counted, because he had done it grudgingly. Oh, it counted for the building fund, but it did not count unto him for righteousness. But he knew he needed to repent of that.

The Lord would have us act with a willing spirit as we sacrifice earthly things. Otherwise, we really are not accepted of him, our faith is decreased, and our spiritual power is weakened. Unwilling attitudes need to be changed that they might be sanctified and made sacred.

When I was serving as a mission president, one of the mission zones had an interesting experience. The zone leaders called all their missionaries the night before Preparation day and said, "We want all of you to meet with us tomorrow morning at 9:30 A.M. at the church in your proselyting clothes." The missionaries asked why but were only told they would find out when they came. The zone leaders simply emphasized that they should all be there.

The next morning all of the missionaries were there, and all were asking why. The zone leaders showed up about fifteen to twenty minutes late. When they arrived, they did not have their materials ready. They were fooling around with one thing or another and even stopped to visit with some of the missionaries. Eventually they started the meeting about forty-five minutes late. Finally, one of the elders asked what was going on. The zone leaders said, "We really didn't have anything particular in mind. We just wanted to have you come over, nothing special." The missionaries replied, "Are you kidding us?" When the zone leaders said they were not kidding, the missionaries said, "This is our P-day. You brought us over here and wasted our time for nothing?" The zone leader said, "Now you know how the Savior feels when you waste His time."

I thought that was a good teaching moment. The missionaries resisted having their time wasted. But time is an earthly thing, and they had already committed to make time a sacred resource in the Lord's work. Whatever He might ask them to do with their time should be all right with them and with all of us.

We can see one of the reasons for the difference between Nephi and his brothers Laman and Lemuel. They all left the comfort of their earthly possessions as they walked away from Jerusalem, but there was a noticeable difference in their willingness to do so that paralleled the noticeable difference in their levels of faith. Though Laman and Lemuel gave up many earthly things, they were obviously not willing to do so. They did the right thing but for the wrong reason. They did not make sacred their response to the Lord's requests. They were not willing to comply with the commandment given by the Lord in our dispensation: "Thou shalt lay aside the things of this world, and seek for the things of a better" (D&C 25:10).

David Whitmer was released from his responsibilities in the ministry by the Lord with this explanation: "Behold, I say unto you, David, that you have feared man and have not relied on me for strength [power from on high] as you ought.

"But your mind has been on the things of the earth more than on the things of me, your Maker, and the ministry whereunto you have been called; and you have not given heed unto my Spirit" (D&C 30:1–2).

2. Giving Away Our Sins. This is a second dimension of the law of sacrifice. In the Book of Mormon, we read a great statement on this subject by a Lamanite king whom Aaron had been teaching: "And it came to pass that when Aaron had said these words, the king did bow down before the Lord, upon his knees; yea, even he did prostrate himself upon the earth, and cried mightily, saying:

"O God, Aaron hath told me that there is a God; and if there is a God, and if thou art God, wilt thou make thyself known unto me, and *I will give away all my sins to know thee,* and that I may be raised from the dead, and be saved at the last day" (Alma 22:17–18; emphasis added).

The king was willing to give away all his sins to know God, or, in other words, he was willing to offer a sacrifice of sin. By doing so, he would make sacred his relationship with God. From John 17:3 we learn that eternal life is to know God. Eternal life is conditioned upon giving away or cleansing ourselves of all unrighteousness. A sacrifice of our sins is a means by which we make sacred our lives and our very nature. That is the pattern for celestial living.

The Savior delivered a celestial sermon when He gave the Sermon on the Mount. He taught people celestial laws and instructed them on how to sacrifice for the development of a celestial nature. The sermon is recorded in Matthew 5–7. A sermon like unto it is also recorded in 3 Nephi 12–14. We will learn from the sermon as it is recorded in the Book of Mormon.

The first verses are referred to as the beatitudes. The first beatitude is recorded in 3 Nephi 12:1. Near the end of the verse it states: "Therefore blessed are ye if ye shall believe in me and be baptized." Baptism is the first level of covenant-making for the covenant people who live in celestial environments, so the first beatitude speaks of blessings for those who are baptized.

The first word of every one of the next ten verses is either "yea" or "and," thereby connecting that verse to the previous one and then back to the first beatitude. Every beatitude is a statement of potential blessing for those who have first been baptized. We read in verse three: "Yea, blessed are the poor in spirit who come unto me." They come unto Him through baptism, and then they are not poor in spirit any more, and theirs is the kingdom of heaven.

In verse four we read: "And again, blessed are all they that mourn, for they shall be comforted." The greatest thing we mourn about is sin. There is nothing more serious than sin to mourn about, so we sacrifice sin and are comforted by the Comforter, or Holy Ghost, which is bestowed upon people who are baptized into the kingdom. We may mourn for other reasons as well, but will still find lasting comfort and inner peace from the Holy Spirit.

Next we read in verse five: "And blessed are the meek, for they shall inherit the earth." The meek are those who have removed pride and arrogance from themselves and become humble and teachable. The earth will be the celestial kingdom, and we must receive and keep sacred our covenants in order to live here.

In verse six it is recorded: "And blessed are all they who do hunger and thirst after righteousness, for they shall be filled with the Holy Ghost." They previously sacrificed sin, were baptized, and continued with lives of righteousness through the spiritual power provided by the Holy Ghost. The result is that they are pure in heart and shall see God (verse 8), even though they may be persecuted because they bear the name of Christ (verse 10).

The whole sermon is a celestial sermon; it is a law of celestial doctrine. It is not a pattern of terrestrial or telestial living. Jesus taught celestial doctrine. Prior to Jesus' coming, the Israelites were under the Mosaic law, which was a terrestrial law, because they could not live a celestial one. Through Moses, the Lord had given them the lesser law, and they had been governed by that law until Jesus completed His ministry. In this sermon, He taught how they could be raised to a celestial level: "Therefore come unto me and be ye saved; for verily I say unto you, that except ye shall keep my commandments, which I have commanded you *at this time,* ye shall in no case enter into the kingdom of heaven" (3 Ne. 12:20; emphasis added).

Giving away sins must be a sacrifice of unrighteousness of the deed as well as wrongful feelings in the heart. In 3 Nephi we read: "Behold, it is written by them of old time [reflecting back to the old law] that thou shalt not commit adultery." Unrepentant adulterers go to the telestial kingdom. To avoid a telestial inheritance, one must not be an adulterer. Then the Savior added: "But I say unto you [and here is the celestial law] that whosoever looketh on a woman, to lust after her, hath committed adultery already in his heart. . . . Suffer none of these things to enter into your heart" (3 Ne. 12:27–29).

There can be no lust in the celestial kingdom. In D&C 63:16 we learn what happens to people who lust. They lose the Spirit. A person who has lust lacks spiritual power and cannot live in a celestial environment. Lust must be sacrificed. We not only must eliminate unrighteous outward acts, but we must also renounce inward conditions that conflict with celestial living. We must make sacred our inner vessel.

Another illustration is found in 3 Nephi 13. The Savior said we should not do alms or pray or fast before men so they know what we are doing (see 3 Ne. 13:1–6). Why? There is nothing wrong with praying, fasting, doing deeds of service, or alms; but be careful about doing the right thing for the wrong reason. What is the sacrifice? The praise of men. What are our motives? We should examine our hearts. The sacrifice is to eliminate those things that hinder the acquisition of spiritual power. Our willingness to do so will bring about an increased capacity to gain access to the powers of heaven.

3. Denial of Self. Let's discuss a third dimension of the law of sacrifice. In Matthew 16:24, we read: "Then said Jesus unto his disciples, If any man will come after me, let him deny himself, and take up his cross, and follow me." What is the sacrifice? The denial of self. President Kimball once said: "Every divorce is the result of selfishness on the part of one or the other or both parties to a marriage contract. Someone is thinking of self-comforts, conveniences, freedoms, luxuries, or ease" (*The Teachings of Spencer W. Kimball,* 313).

Whenever there is contention between two people, the biggest obstacle to the solution is selfishness. That is true with missionary companions, marriages, friends, and neighbors. We must be willing to sacrifice self-interests and self-serving activities that cause sadness or sorrow for someone else. The greatest key to building a good relationship is to be willing to be selfless in that relationship. Look to the needs of others.

A young lady was crying when she came home from a date one night. When her mother asked why the tears and what in the world was the matter, she said, "I don't think he had a good time." Her concern came from a selfless heart.

The concept of a selfish lifestyle is often seen in dating and courtship. Many young people grow up being selfish. Generally, when they consider whom to date, they decide according to self-satisfying criteria. Others have a more enlightened view.

I remember three young men who were seniors in high school. One was the student body president, one was president of the Seminary, and the other was a star athlete. All were outstanding Latter-day Saint students. They decided they would ask girls who had never dated in their lives to accompany them to their senior prom. They bought them flowers, took them to a very nice restaurant, and had a wonderful evening together at the dance. Those young women would ever treasure that marvelous evening and a most memorable experience that had been provided just for them. Caring about others is a Christlike attribute to be sought for and developed through the deliberate and willing sacrifice of self-serving quests.

Young people should learn to be selfless before they go to the temple to get married. They need to practice selflessness in the development and creation of proper relationships with the opposite sex. For instance, sexual deviation is a manifestation of selfish behavior. While dating, there is a need to protect and defend the spiritual well-being of others while striving to provide opportunity for their happiness. This is Christlike behavior and perfect preparation for marriage. An eternal marriage is based on a commitment to live the selfless commandment, "Thou shalt love thy wife [or thy husband] with all thy heart" (D&C 42:22).

Missionaries, young as well as senior, fit all three dimensions of the law of sacrifice. A true missionary is willing to give up all earthly things to serve the Lord on a mission. Secondly, interviews with the bishop and stake president help determine if there has been a sacrifice of sin or unrighteousness. Third, a missionary is called to serve someone else. Certainly there are many personal benefits from the service, but that is not the motive. The purpose in serving is to share the gospel with others. When people come into this Church as new converts, the first thing they want to do is share the gospel and be selfless with it. That is what Lehi experienced in his dream. After he partook of the fruit of the tree, he looked around for others and beckoned for them to come and enjoy the delicious fruit of the Atonement (see 1 Ne. 8:12–17). Enos obtained forgiveness from the Lord and then pled with the Lord for the souls of others, including his enemies (see Enos 1:5–11). The sons of Mosiah experienced a spiritual rebirth and then sought for the opportunity to share their newly found feelings with their Lamanite enemies (see Mosiah 28:1–3). John the Revelator and the three Nephite disciples all desired to stay on the earth and bring souls unto the Savior for as long as the world should stand (see D&C 7:2 and 3 Ne. 28:6, 9).

Can we see the Savior in these three dimensions of the law? First, what were the conditions of His birth? We read Nephi's description of the condescension of the Savior (see 1 Ne. 11:26–33). He had been a King, a God, a Creator, yet He was willing to relinquish His status and position and descend to a lowly place of mortality, where people ridiculed Him, smote upon Him, mocked Him, judged Him, and crucified Him. And He let them. Next, He avoided all unrighteousness while maintaining a sacred relationship with His Father. Third, He gave His life while ministering, suffering, and dying for others. We cannot read any passages in holy writ that describe Him doing anything for Himself. He had the power to do all things in righteousness, including power over sin and death. Perhaps we see more clearly what He meant when He said, "Follow me, and I will make you fishers of men" (Matt. 4:19).

We learn a lot about ourselves when we ask ourselves these questions: Do I have a broken heart and a contrite spirit? Why am I doing what I am doing? Am I selfish or selfless? Each of us has to wrestle with these issues because that is the law of sacrifice in the gospel of Jesus Christ. This is His law; it is for our benefit, that we might possess souls that have been made sacred.

President David O. McKay encapsulated this law and doctrine in the following marvelous teaching:

> Every noble impulse, every unselfish expression of love, every brave suffering for the right; every surrender of self to something higher than self; every loyalty to an ideal; every unselfish devotion to principle; every helpfulness to humanity; every act of self-control; every fine courage of the soul, undefeated by pretense or policy, but by being, doing, and living of good for the very good's sake—that is spirituality. . . . Spirituality, our true aim, is the consciousness of victory over self and of communion with the Infinite. Spirituality impels one to conquer difficulties and acquire more and more strength. To feel one's faculties unfolding and truth expanding the soul is one of life's most sublime experiences. Would that all might so live as to experience that ecstasy! (CR, Oct. 1956, 5–6).

All who live the Lord's law of sacrifice enjoy an increasing amount of spirituality. They are free from the encumbrances of earthly things, consequences of unrighteousness, and the binding cords of selfishness. They make sacred their souls through the sanctifying and enabling power from on high.

CHAPTER 12
THE HEALING POWER

As a prelude to our discussion on the healing power, I want to share something that became apparent to me years ago. I knew that I needed to study the scriptures with a different approach, and not just seek answers to questions like "what, who, when, and where" as a means of obtaining and learning gospel teachings. I knew that was not satisfactory; it was not adequate. I felt there was a dimension missing, so I began to explore answers to "why" questions. I used the why-type questions more than any others. Though the other questions are vital to the building of an informational scaffold, answers to them do not serve the purpose of explaining reasons why the material has been provided. After all, scriptures come out of the historic past and will be of greatest value when we understand how to apply the principles that are pertinent for our use today.

For instance, I asked questions like, why do we need to know certain things? Or why did a prophet choose to write what he did? Or why have certain scriptural statements been prepared for us to read in our day? With that questioning technique in mind, I will ask a three-word question starting with *why*. Why not sin? Let me give a reason why we should be prepared to answer that. I remember Elder Spencer W. Kimball observing, "Whoever said that sin is not fun?" (CR, Apr. 1961, 66). Of course, sin must be enticing or we would not do it. And we all do. We surely would not work at it. It must have some appeal. It attracts people all over the earth and catches all of us sometimes. There are many reasons to sin. We need reasons *not* to sin.

Let me share a few illustrations. I remember a man who was an advisor to an Aaronic Priesthood teachers quorum. He came to me and asked about a problem he was experiencing. Some of the teachers in the quorum were smoking. One of the presidency was the ringleader of the group. He said he had talked with all of them as a group and individually, but had not been able to get through to them. He asked for suggestions. I said, "Well, let me guess what you have tried so far. You have probably told them not to smoke because it shortens life. But that did not matter to them. Besides, one of them may have a loved one who smoked all his life and lived to a ripe old age. Maybe you have talked to them about being great athletes, and told them they shouldn't smoke because it will hinder their athletic ability. But one of the boys probably knows of a seven-digit salary athlete who uses tobacco, so you are getting nowhere. The boys are raising the question, 'Why not smoke?'"

Some years ago a young returned missionary came to get his temple recommend signed. I asked him all the questions. When it came to the question about being morally clean, I explained to him what it means to be morally clean. His response was, "I am doing fine in everything except petting. But I don't do that with anybody except my fiancée. I don't understand what is wrong with that as long as it is just with her. We are going to be married in a month anyway, so why not pet?"

I am acquainted with a good man, a fine family man and a member of the Church, but he does not attend sacrament meetings. Why not? He said, "Each time I have gone, I have missed seeing a good ball game. In our chapel we have hard pews to sit on, and at home I have a nice comfortable chair. At home I have a fireplace, refreshments, and I am far more comfortable. I enjoy my Sundays much more at home than I ever have at church. Besides, I have heard it preached that families are first. So, I stay home and enjoy my family. Why not?"

I don't know if there are these kinds of problems in every stake or family, but I suspect it is not an uncommon set of circumstances. We all deal with this question at some time or another and must face the question, "Why not sin?" So we need help, and I propose that we discover answers from the Lord.

When our family was young, we loved to go camping. One time we took our camp trailer into the mountains, and after it was all set up, my wife suggested that the children and I go for a hike while she prepared food for us. Since we had not been in this area before, it was exploring time so we wandered up into the hills and came to a beautiful mountain stream. We wanted to be on the other side since it seemed to be more appealing over there, but crossing the stream would not be an easy task. It was wide and deep enough to make it difficult to cross. I walked up and down the stream to see if there was a place where it was narrow enough to jump or perhaps find some rocks that we might step on and get across. I thought there might be a tree that had fallen across the stream that we could crawl on. None of those options were available.

Finally, I found a small tree lying alongside the bank that would span the stream and accommodate our weight. All we had to do was stand it up on one end, let it fall across the stream, and then we could crawl over. There was just one little problem. The tree was on the other side! But the plan would work if I could get over there and tip it over. Then the children could cross on it.

I found a place where I thought the stream was narrow enough that I could jump it. I calculated that if I had a good run I could leap the stream. I found a place on the stream bank that would serve as a launch pad where I could plant my foot and leap across to a spot on the other bank. So I tried it. I reached the other side, but fell backwards into the water. I put my left hand down to stop my fall. My hand went to the bottom of the stream into an assortment of rocks, sharp sticks, and sand. As my hand hit the bottom I felt the skin pop open between the thumb and the forefinger and soon discovered exposed bone and bleeding flesh.

I climbed out of the stream and headed back to the trailer. As we approached, my wife looked at my dripping wet condition and asked what had happened. I explained and said I had come to get a Band-Aid. When she saw my bleeding thumb, she decided we needed professional medical assistance.

We were able to find a doctor in the nearest town. He said he would need to clean it out and began to probe around a bit while pouring in some kind of liquid. That really hurt. He used some tweezers and picked out some foreign matter, wiped out the wound, poured in additional liquid, probed some more, and wiped it out again. I said to him, "I'll be glad when you quit that!" He said, "I can quit, but I'm not quite through. I can bandage it and send you home, but when you come back next week it will be swollen and infected and extremely sore. Now, do you want me to continue or do you want me to stop?" I thought about that and then said, "Well, okay, do it, but hurry!" I don't think he hurried, but he finally finished. He medicated, sewed, and bandaged it and then said, "Now, you go home but don't use that hand. I don't want anything happening to the stitches. Don't grip anything with it and don't get it wet. You come back in a week, and we'll check it over and see how it is doing." A week later I went back, and he took out the stitches. It soon healed and today it is okay, though I still have a visible scar.

Now the reason for the story. What I just related about my thumb is what happens when we sin, but instead of the physical body being injured, the spirit is. Sin causes spiritual wounds, and the healing process is basically the same as for physical ones. We do not ignore physical wounds, and we can't ignore spiritual ones either. They have to heal. The reason is that there will be no resurrection to any degree of glory for anyone until their sin-caused wounds are healed. There are no exceptions. We have no more choice as to whether the wounds are healed than we have a choice as to whether we will be resurrected. We will all be resurrected, and except for sons of perdition, all spiritual wounds will be healed. (See D&C 88:21–24, 35.)

We do have a choice as to *how* the wound is healed. The Lord revealed that choice very clearly when He said: "And surely every man must repent or suffer" (D&C 19:4). Why every man? In Romans 3:23 we read that all have sinned. If all have sinned, then all must repent or suffer. Only one person ever lived on this earth who avoided blemishes or wounds from sin, and that was Christ. We remember that Peter referred to Him as a lamb without blemish or spot (see 1 Pet. 1:19). There were no blemishes on His soul, no spots, no wounds, because there were no sins to cause such. All other accountable people have sinned and are blemished or wounded.

We can choose which process we want to heal our wounds—repent or suffer. Listen to the Savior's admonition concerning our choice. In D&C 19:13 we read, "Wherefore, I command you to repent." In verse 15, He said: "Therefore I command you to repent." In verse 20, He said: "Wherefore, I command you again to repent." Is there any doubt as to which choice the Lord thinks is best? He thinks we should choose to repent. What is the result of repentance? The Lord will teach us the ultimate objective of repentance and then show us how we get there.

Let's hear what the Savior said to the Nephites after His Resurrection but before He appeared to them. The very fact that it is in His first sermon to them gives us a sense of the priority value of the information. From the heavens came His words: "O all ye that are spared because ye were more righteous than they, will ye not now return unto me, and *repent of your sins,* and be converted, *that I may heal you?*" (3 Ne. 9:13; emphasis added).

He will heal spiritual wounds, but repentance is required for us to gain access to the healing power of the Atonement of Jesus Christ. That power comes from on high, which is the reason why repentance is the best choice.

What really happens when we repent? First, we must be aware that there has been an injury. No one repents until he realizes there is a wound. Then we begin to do what is needed to start the healing process. Sometimes, spiritual wounds are Band-Aid size. They may be minimal. Deep wounds do not come from small sinful incidents. We are able to handle those directly with the Lord. It is like taking over-the-counter medication or bandaging a small knee scrape.

But like the torn flesh around my thumb, deep wounds of the spirit require physician assistance. Some may not know we have such help in the Church. In D&C 31:10, the Lord referred to Thomas B. Marsh as "a physician unto the church." When keys of judgment are given to a priesthood holder, he becomes a physician unto the Church. Bishops and stake and mission presidents all serve in that role as people we go to for help in getting wounds healed. Spiritual physicians in the Church do not heal spiritual wounds any more than medical doctors heal physical ones. They help us experience whatever is necessary for healing to occur. When we visit with spiritual physicians, the first thing we must do is expose the wound. The scriptures speak of that as confession. Exposing the wound includes identifying and cleaning out matters that are foreign to spiritual cleanliness, anything that would be offensive to the Spirit. We remove things from the soul that prevent the wound from being healed.

It is not a pleasant experience for a person to go through. He may find himself sitting in the office of a bishop and, while exposing wounds, thinking to himself, "This is really painful. I will be glad when this is over." But what if he exposes only part of it? What if he stops before he gets it all out? Will it heal? No. Just like the thumb, it will remain infected. Spiritual abscesses do not heal without treatment. Our spiritual physician may say, "I know this is painful for you, but it is the only way. Let me help you so the wounds can heal." Maybe he will decide to limit or restrict our actions or behavior for a time. Maybe he will prescribe repeat visits. Maybe he will suggest some spiritual medicine that will help us be more spiritually responsive to the healing powers from on high.

One of the more commonly asked questions of a spiritual physician is, "How long will it take?" He does not know. That depends on many factors, like the depth of the wound, how well we cleanse it, and how carefully we follow directions and counsel given by our spiritual physician. Then, when we have done all we should and could, we appeal for the Lord to apply the healing power of the Atonement, and the wound is healed. The bishop does not know how long that will take. But we know when it is healed because the mental, emotional, and spiritual pain is gone. We recall what Alma said: "I could remember my pains no more" (Alma 36:19). Though he could remember his sinful experience, the pain associated with his repentance was gone. He knew he was healed.

For King Benjamin's people there was a "peace of conscience" (see Mosiah 4:3), which is precisely what was missing with one dear sister. After discussing these same principles with her, she said to me, "I wish I had heard this twenty years ago when I was involved in some immoral experiences. I told no one except my mother. She chastised me in ways that I could not even imagine. She threatened me almost with my life if I should ever do that again. I remember asking her if I needed to talk to our bishop. Her answer was, 'I should say not. It's none of his business. You just see that you never do that again, young lady.' I never did. I also did not even discuss it with the Lord. For twenty years, I have never felt any peace, but I did not know why until now."

Enos described his feelings with this declaration: "My guilt was swept away" (Enos 1:6). Those are descriptive words and phrases that are used to describe how people feel after the healing is complete. The Savior said He could heal us, and He does.

There is another factor we should discuss. I remember a young lady who came in to see me one day. She said, "There is something I need to talk about. I'm engaged to a fine young man, but we have had some petting problems, even though we have not wanted that to happen. We know better, but it has happened two or three times. Each time, we have gone to the bishop and explained to him what we have done, and told him that we are sorry. We really are sorry; we regret our actions each time. Now it has happened again, and I don't know what to do. I am embarrassed to go back to the bishop. He is not going to believe that we are trying. I wondered if you had any suggestions as to what we can do. Is there anything that will help us?" I told her I was not sure, but would tell her what came to mind. The following experience was what I shared with her.

Some years ago I was out early one morning in the summertime working on my truck. I felt something break loose inside my head. It hit hard and kept getting more painful. After a few minutes I went into the house and for the next few hours went through an experience that was later discovered to be a ruptured blood vessel in my head, known as an aneurysm. Our high priest neighbor came over and gave me a blessing, but there was no noticeable physical relief.

Ultimately, I ended up in a hospital. While there, a neurosurgeon determined he needed to measure some pressure differentials inside my head by inserting a very long needle into the brain while watching on an X-ray machine. He explained that I needed to be conscious so I could respond as he proceeded with the test. He could anesthetize only the area right around the needle, which would help, but it would still be very painful.

He was right. He began to insert the needle, and each time he moved it at all, it felt like the probe was on fire. I have never experienced a more painful ordeal. He kept going further and further until I could no longer endure it. I told him I could not tolerate any more and he needed to take the needle out, which he did. I determined I would never go through such an experience again. Though blood was found in the spinal column, the aneurysm had miraculously healed over as a result of the priesthood blessing, and I recovered.

I asked the young lady if she could learn anything from my experience. I told her that according to Alma 42:16, there is no repentance without punishment, or in other words, suffering, hurting, and sorrow. Forgiveness is not free or easy. We don't simply say we are sorry and promise not to do it again. Perhaps there had not been adequate sorrow or enough hurt; maybe the heart had not been sufficiently broken to determine the sin would not happen again. Proper repentance prevents repetition. With new understanding, the couple sought for and obtained the power to prevent their having any more problems. Their nature needed to change. There needed to be "no more disposition to do evil, but to do good continually" (Mosiah 5:2).

Sometimes a benefit resulting from Church discipline is deeper sorrow and a stronger determination to bring about a reformation in life. Sometimes people do not suffer enough on their own to gain access to the healing power of the Atonement, so do not ever reach the necessary level of eligibility for forgiveness. Inspired physicians of the priesthood tell us what we need to do to obtain the Savior's mercy, and that becomes part of the prescription process for healing.

There is another factor that we read about in D&C 58:43. It mentions how man may know if he has repented of his sins. He will confess them before God and forsake them. What does it mean to forsake? Consider the first of two parts. What if I were to return to that same mountain stream, try to jump it, fall in, and tear the flesh near my thumb again? I would have another wounding experience, and my thumb would be the same as if it had never healed. The Savior said, "Unto that soul who sinneth shall the former sins return" (D&C 82:7). We must not go back to sin and its wounding effects. Many people labor under the impression that once forgiveness is obtained, it is permanent. It may not be. We have only reached a conditional level that may also be temporary. King Benjamin taught that not only must we obtain forgiveness, we must retain it (see Mosiah 4:11–12, 26). We must continue to live worthy of the healing. If we do not, wounds are opened again as though they had not been healed. We must forsake sin; otherwise, we are burdened with unhealed wounds.

Here is the second part. When we sin, the Spirit leaves. Forsaking sins must not only be a physical forsaking, but also a mental one. Once we have obtained forgiveness, we can only retain it if we forsake the sinful experience mentally. Suppose we do not, but instead, from time to time, we rehearse in our minds the sins of the past. It doesn't make much difference to our spiritual condition if we are thinking about sin in anticipation or in reflection. Either way, we lose the Spirit as a result of such thoughts. Forsaking sin must be mental as well.

One of the Savior's prophets described the results of following the Lord's counsel to repent. Isaiah wrote of the coming and Atonement of the Messiah about seven centuries before His birth. In Isaiah 53:4-5, Isaiah speaks as though it had already happened, for in his mind it had. He had visualized it. It had been revealed to him as prophetic history. Of the Savior's redemption he wrote: ". . . he has borne our griefs, and carried our sorrows: . . . he was wounded for our transgressions." He took upon Himself the burdens of sins, but none of them were His own. The wounds He carried were inflicted by our sins. He was wounded for what we did: "He was bruised for our iniquities; the chastisement of our peace was upon him; and with his stripes we are healed."

When Enos sought forgiveness, he prayed all day and into the night. Eventually, he obtained it. He was told, "Thy sins are forgiven. . . . Thy faith hath made thee whole" (Enos 1:5, 8). What had been made whole? His spirit body. His soul had been made whole. There were no more wounds, no more blemishes, and no more spots. They were all healed. There were no scars, either. That is one of the miraculous parts of spiritual healing.

We have all heard that sin is like driving a nail into a board, and repentance is like pulling the nail out again. But the hole in the board is still there. What kind of healing would that be? Perhaps we could use that analogy if we modified it a bit. The wood in the board must grow back and be restored to its whole or complete condition. The Lord causes things to happen that we have no power to bring about. It is my faith that Jesus Christ has the power to do so.

We have seen the result of choosing repentance. What was the other choice? The alternative was to suffer. We read in D&C 19:4, "And surely every man must repent or suffer." Suppose I choose not to repent because I think it doesn't matter. I think I do not have to repent; no one can force me to do so. Maybe no one knows what I have done, and I do not have to tell anyone. I may think I can hide it. Adam tried to hide from God when his transgression occurred. It didn't work! (See Moses 4:14.) Hiding is a bad choice. For instance, the Lord said early in this dispensation, "Let that which has been bestowed upon Ziba Peterson be taken from him . . . until he is sufficiently chastened for all his sins; for he confesseth them not, and thinketh to hide them" (D&C 58:60). From whom can we hide sins? Maybe we can hide from the bishop, stake or mission president, wife, or husband. Perhaps we could successfully do so as long as we live in this mortal body. No one can see the blemishes on the spirit.

In our deepest recesses of thought, though, we must consider that the Lord already knows. But then we may think He is a God of mercy and everything will eventually be all right. We may conclude that someday, when we are not here to face friends and family, it will be easier to handle. So, why not?

But what happens when we die? The spirit leaves the protective, covering veil of its mortal body. Might our blemishes and wounds be visible? If we remember reading D&C 88:108–109, we know that the secret acts of men will be revealed. There will be no secrets. Suppose unhealed wounds exist because the person, though he had been taught and knew the gospel, chose not to repent. He thought he would hide his sins, which he did while in mortality. For him comes the alternative—suffering. Let's read about suffering.

> I command you to repent—repent, lest I smite you by the rod of my mouth, and by my wrath, and by my anger, and your sufferings be sore—how sore you know not, how exquisite you know not, yea, how hard to bear you know not.
>
> For behold, I, God, have suffered these things for all, that they might not suffer if they would repent;
>
> But if they would not repent they must suffer even as I;
>
> Which suffering caused myself, even God, the greatest of all, to tremble because of pain. . . .
>
> Wherefore, I command you again to repent, lest I humble you with my almighty power; and that you confess your sins, lest you suffer these punishments of which I have spoken, of which in the smallest, yea, even in the least degree you have tasted at the time I withdrew my spirit (D&C 19:15–18, 20).

Why did Jesus Christ bleed from every pore when He was wounded for our transgressions? Brigham Young said it was because the Holy Spirit was withdrawn from Him (see *JD*, 3:206). That makes a lot of sense to all of us who have sinned. We know that when sin occurs, when wounding takes place, the Spirit leaves. Well, if Jesus was wounded because He was bearing sins, even though they were not His own, naturally the Spirit would leave. For the first time in His life, this supersensitive, spiritual soul found Himself being forsaken by the Spirit, and He was spiritually alone. He bled from every pore because the pain of sin was so intense, and He was without the Comforter.

When we die, we will find ourselves outside of the protective veil of our mortal body. If we have previously chosen not to repent, then our blemished spirit will still need to be healed. So we go to a spirit hospital in a spirit prison. The scriptures also call it outer darkness or hell (see Moses 6:29). Those who have chosen not to repent, have, by default, chosen to suffer, and will find themselves in a spirit world environment of outer darkness where the Spirit is not. There they go through the process of being healed through their own suffering—alone, and without the Spirit. Thus, they suffer even as Christ did without the power of the Holy Spirit, though they do not suffer even a minuscule amount of the intensity and magnitude of pain that He did. Except for the sons of perdition, all will come out of their suffering experience, clean and without wounds; but remember, those people did not previously have enough faith in Christ and chose not to repent. They did not have enough faith to be obedient, thereby preventing the acquisition and development of sufficient spiritual power that would enable them to return to the presence of God and His celestial environment. So, though they are healed, they end up in a lesser degree of glory.

Which of the two courses of action is pleasant—repentance or suffering? Neither. Repentance is decidedly better than the other and is the best choice. But neither process is pleasant. A mandatory healing experience is a consequence of sin. And regardless of which way we choose to obtain the healing, it is not enjoyable.

Do we now have an answer to the question, why not sin? There is an attendant wounding that accompanies every willful act of disobedience against the commandments of God. Wounds are caused by petting, choosing to be absent from sacrament meetings, breaking the Word of Wisdom, or any of the many other things we might do to break our covenants with God, and all wounds must be healed.

There is still another dimension to our discussion that the Lord has revealed. The early Saints in Ohio had been thinking and talking about going to Missouri, but they were chastised by the Lord because they had talked critically about Joseph Smith, their prophet-leader. In D&C 64:6–7 it is recorded that the Lord said to them: "There are those who have sought occasion against him without cause; Nevertheless, he has sinned; [of course he has; he is a mortal being] but verily I say unto you, I, the Lord, forgive sins."

Do we know of any announcement ever made in this world that has greater impact upon us? Yet, the Lord would never impose forgiveness upon anyone. Individual agency would be disregarded if He did. He is not like Lucifer, who has no respect for agency. The devil has sought from the beginning to control a person's privilege of choosing. He comes into our lives uninvited, whereas the Lord does not and would not. Those who seek forgiveness may obtain it, but the Lord honors their right to refrain from asking.

Our great Master Teacher then shared a principle with all Saints in the latter days. He illustrated it from a previous period of time and another people. In D&C 64:8–9, he said: "My disciples, in days of old, sought occasion against one another and forgave not one another in their hearts; and for this evil [notice what he called their failure to forgive one another] they were afflicted." Afflicted? How? Where? It surely was not a physical affliction, was it? Though they were not the trespassers, they were non-forgivers. Thus they were afflicted, which means wounded. The ones who failed to forgive were afflicted. Further we read, "Wherefore, I say unto you, that ye ought to forgive one another; for he that forgiveth not his brother his trespasses standeth condemned before the Lord; for there remaineth in him the greater sin."

The Savior did not say they had failed to forgive a brother of his sins. People do not sin against each other. We sin against the Lord. We trespass against one another. We do not forgive sins of one another, because there are no sins for us to forgive. Only the Savior forgives sin. He alone suffered and atoned for sins, so we take our sins to Him. Though we are not healers of sinners, we should be forgivers of trespassers who cause us to be hurt or offended. There remains in the non-forgiver a greater sin than the trespass of one person against another.

The Lord goes on to say, "I, the Lord, will forgive whom I will forgive." That is very conditional. Forgiveness by the Lord depends on repentance, faith, obedience, and all the other things we have talked about. Then He continues, "but of you it is required to forgive all men" (verse 10). There are no exceptions and no conditions.

May I suggest that we consider what the Lord did not say? He did not say, "Of you it is required to forgive all men after you get even." Nor did he say that we should forgive all men "if they are sorry," or "if they repent," or "after they suffer."

There are no conditions in the requirement for us to forgive each other. It does not depend on the seriousness of the transgression or the degree of sorrow in the heart of the transgressor. There are no conditions. Of us it is required to forgive all men, regardless of what they may have done. It is for our good; otherwise feelings against another person can be spiritually devastating and hinder our spiritual receptivity. Elder Marion D. Hanks shared the following:

It is reported that President Brigham Young once said that he who takes offense when no offense was intended is a fool, and he who takes offense when offense was intended is usually a fool. It was then explained that there are two courses of action to follow when one is bitten by a rattlesnake. One may, in anger, fear, or vengefulness, pursue the creature and kill it. Or he may make full haste to get the venom out of his system. If we pursue the latter course we will likely survive, but if we attempt to follow the former, we may not be around long enough to finish it (CR, Oct. 1973, 16).

It can be and often is very difficult to resolve offenses, particularly if there is a confusion of terms. Let me illustrate. A number of years ago, a couple came to discuss a problem that had surfaced in their marriage. She had been unfaithful to her husband on a number of occasions while living under the covenants of a temple marriage. He had not known that such things were going on. Finally, she could not live like that any more. She hated her behavior and herself for doing it. She went to her husband and to the Church authorities. The wound was exposed so it might be healed and she could be cleansed. In this case, the discipline system of the Church was utilized to help her, and she was excommunicated. Her husband loved her and wanted to keep their family together and maintain family integrity, so they were working at rebuilding their marriage, though it was a very difficult thing to do.

One day they came to my office and asked for counsel. She said, "I don't think we are ever going to be able to put our marriage back together." I asked her why she felt that way. Her response was, "You can't build a marriage where there isn't trust." I agreed and asked her to explain. "Well," she said, "as you know, I work and don't get off work the same time every day. Sometimes I'm a little late finishing; sometimes I don't get away from work for ten, fifteen, or thirty minutes, and by the time I get home, my husband is worrying that I may be with some man again. Or if I go to the store or run an errand and he doesn't know where I am at the time, he worries that I am involved in wrongdoing. If the phone rings and I don't mention to him who called or what the message was about, he thinks I'm talking to somebody privately and making secret arrangements. He just doesn't trust me."

Essentially, I expressed the following to her: "Well, I understand what you're saying, and I can only partially appreciate how much you are hurting because of what you've been through and what you are now experiencing. I can only imagine that hurt, but I do empathize. I would like you to listen very carefully to the things I want to say to you. You are aware, I am sure, that your husband is a man of God. In D&C 42:22 we read of a commandment to your husband, 'Thou shalt love thy wife with all thy heart,' and he does. Your husband is also under a divine mandate to forgive you, and he has, but you must understand something else. Your husband is not under any divine directive to trust you, and right now, he doesn't. That is your fault, not his. Trust is what you destroyed, but must restore as a part of the process of restitution. You are responsible to recreate trust. That is not his burden; it is yours. You must not be late coming home from work without letting him know what is happening. Even if it costs you your job, it would be better than losing your marriage. Don't go to the store without his knowing where you are, when you are going, and when you will return. When phone calls come, you make an effort to tell him who called or what the conversation was about, so he does not have to ask or wonder. You must initiate that kind of an effort. You must go out of your way to be sure there is no room for doubt, no reason why he should have questions. You must make the effort to recreate trust. It can be rebuilt, but it will take time. I know that will not be easy, but you can do it."

She understood and went away with a renewed commitment to make the necessary effort. Her husband had also been confused. He was feeling guilty because he thought maybe he truly had not forgiven her, or maybe he did not love her as he should. That was not the issue at all. It was a trust-level problem that they both needed to understand. We are commanded to love and forgive, but trust must be earned. The Lord loves all of His children, but surely is unable to trust all of them. President David O. McKay taught a great principle when he said, "To be trusted is a greater compliment than to be loved" (*Stepping Stones to an Abundant Life*, 176).

I want to share part of a letter that reinforces the principles of which we have spoken. This letter was written to me by a woman who had been through some very difficult times and years of her life. She had resolved a major conflict by responding favorably to divine counsel, and many other problems were subsequently resolved. She wrote this letter to me and said she wanted me to have it for whatever use or benefit it might be to somebody else. Her name is withheld.

She wrote, "When I was young, I was repeatedly molested and abused. Fear and undeserved guilt kept me quiet for five years. Then, it was twelve more years before I received any professional help. By then the scars had affected me more than I realized. It affected my relationship with my husband, and it contributed to frequent severe depression and suicidal tendencies. Many months of counseling did not solve the problem. One day as I read the scriptures and prayed, my answer came. The best therapy for me was to forgive the man who had inflicted it upon me. That sounded crazy to me. I could see forgiving someone who asked for forgiveness or even someone who halfway deserved it, but the man had done the same thing to dozens of girls, including his own daughter. Why should I forgive him? Besides, he had died a few months earlier. What good would it do him? Then the thought came, 'It isn't for him.' It would be for my benefit. I had bound myself in emotional chains of guilt, anger, hatred, and fear, though I had repressed them from myself so they took form in other ways. Before I could free myself of these so I could progress, it was necessary to forgive him in my heart. That was difficult. It took lots of prayer, but gradually I succeeded. But I had to take it a step further. I also had to forgive myself and release the guilt. The process has been slow. I still have a ways to go, but the bad dreams and other problems have almost completely gone. I have learned that God is the best therapist. He is all-knowing. He cares more than anyone else, and with Him, we have no time limitations and He doesn't charge eighty dollars for fifty minutes. Even the poorest of men can afford the best of care."

Elder Dallin H. Oaks commented on the importance of forgiving others with these insightful comments: "One of the most Godlike expressions of the human soul is the act of forgiveness. Everyone is wronged at some point by someone, and many suffer serious wrongs. . . . Forgiveness is mortality's mirror image of the mercy of God" (CR, Oct. 1989, 81). Unconditional forgiveness of others permits us to avoid self-inflicted blemishes and provides freedom from the false assumption that we can determine if and when an offender should be forgiven.

There is another assumption that merits a comment. Many of us who repent and obtain forgiveness from the Lord assume that when He said He forgives sins and remembers them no more, He means that He forgets them as well. (See D&C 58:42.) A God who has all knowledge does not have lapses of memory. He will remember our sins *to us* no more. He will not bring them to our attention or allow them to influence our relationship with Him. A supporting statement is found in Ezekiel 18:22, where we read that when sins are forgiven "they shall not be mentioned unto him [the sinner] again."

One final observation. In the last chapter of the Book of Mormon, we read Moroni's emphasis on this vital and important subject. All of us have participated in discussions about the Lord's statement in 3 Nephi 12:48. He said, "Be perfect even as I, or your Father who is in heaven is perfect." Many of us talk to each other about whether perfection is possible and conclude that it is not because none of us are. We may justify our imperfections by assuming that perfection is unattainable. Haven't we all heard people say that no one is perfect and no one can be? That raises a strange question. Why would Jesus tell us to become something that is not possible? He was talking to mortals when he made the statement. A better way for us to reason would be to assume it must be possible, or He would not have directed it. With that assumption, we should find a way to reach that level.

Moroni teaches us how it can be. In Moroni 10:32, we read, "Yea, come unto Christ." This is the oft-repeated invitation of The Church of Jesus Christ of Latter-day Saints. Though generally unspoken, there is a connected vital reason for coming to Him.

Come unto Christ, *and be perfected in him,* and deny yourselves of all ungodliness; and if ye shall deny yourselves of all ungodliness, and love God with all your might, mind, and strength, then is his grace sufficient for you, that by his grace *ye may be perfect in Christ;* and if by the grace of God ye are *perfect in Christ,* ye can in nowise deny the power of God.

And again, if ye by the grace of God are *perfect in Christ,* and deny not his power, then are ye sanctified in Christ by the grace of God, through the shedding of the blood of Christ, which is in the covenant of the Father unto the

remission of your sins, that ye become holy, without spot
(Moro. 10:32–33; emphasis added).

We can be perfectly free from the consequences of sin. Through
the Savior's Atonement, we can be perfectly free from blemishes and
wounds caused by sin. We can be perfectly clean, sanctified, and whole
through His Atonement. We can become perfect in Him and be
without blemish and without spot.

God grant that we may seek and attain that level of perfection.
We cannot obtain perfection the way the Savior did, for He kept all
of Father's commandments, and we have already failed to be totally
obedient. But we can become perfect in Him because He redeemed
us from our sins and their consequences.

After quoting the Savior, who said, "Be ye therefore perfect"
(Matt. 5:48), President Spencer W. Kimball wrote: "Being perfect
means to triumph over sin. This is a mandate from the Lord. He is
just and wise and kind. He would never require anything from His
children which was not for their benefit and which was not attainable. Perfection therefore is an achievable goal" (*Miracle of
Forgiveness,* 209).

God help us to choose not to sin—but, failing in that, may we
then choose to repent of our sins that the Lord may heal our
wounds for us. Thus, through the Savior's Atonement, we may gain
access to His healing power from on high by which that miracle
takes place. Untold numbers of people have borne witness that they
have felt the healing powers of the Master and they know that
power is real. May we strive to merit the blessing of peace in Christ.

CHAPTER 13
THE POWER OF PROPHETIC INSIGHTS ON DEATH

Positive expectations of life hereafter offer real hope in the face of death. Latter-day Saints are blessed to have solid hopes of the hereafter through insights from prophets. And those insights are proclaimed and received by an accompanying witness of the Spirit, providing spiritual and sustaining power from on high that strengthens individuals and solidifies their faith. Prophets not only hold out that hope to us, but offer answers to corollary questions: Where do spirits go when their bodies die? What might they do there? What conditions exist in the afterlife?

When death knocks, a door opens permitting spirits to leave their mortal bodies and physical environments. They pass from the view of friends, family members, loved ones, and even strangers who are left behind who wonder what new associations and conditions are being discovered by the departed persons.

I remember my own reaction to death as I stood in a cemetery on a wintry day many years ago. My father had passed away, and it was the day of his funeral and burial. The day seemed even colder than the freezing temperatures; I felt an inward chill as I looked down into the waiting space of an open grave. Earlier that day I had watched the casket close over the beloved form of my dear dad. I watched now as that terribly impersonal box was lowered into the cold earth and covered by the soil that cut off all visual contact and prevented any further physical connection with him.

I realized at that time of trauma that my feelings about his death, as well as others that surely would occur in my lifetime, depended on two things: my memories and my expectations. Since that time, I have mentally and emotionally visited my personal memories as they are recorded in photographs and written entries, but mostly in my mind and heart. I have also searched through recorded teachings of the Lord's prophets on the subject of death, that my expectations might harmonize with revealed truths.

Experiences with death continue to infiltrate my family, friends, and associates. But renewing pleasant memories and reviewing words of explanation and insight from prophets have helped me through confrontations with death, enabling me to refine my focus. There has been an expansion of my understanding of the role of death, with its accompanying conditions and consequences, in Father's plan. And on an emotional level there has been a noticeable and welcome presence of peace that has helped to replace pain.

MEMORIES

Remembering good things about good people is a good thing to do. The Book of Mormon features frequent prophetic counsel about remembering. The prophet Lehi exhorted his children to "Remember the words of thy dying father" (2 Ne. 3:25). He might also have counseled them to remember his love, his kindness, his smile, his work, and his faith in and love of the Lord.

Memories of people from the past are constantly recalled to bring about desirable purposes in the lives of the living. Helaman reminded his sons: ". . . I have given unto you the names of our first parents who came out of the land of Jerusalem; and this I have done that when you remember your names ye may remember them; and when ye remember them ye may remember their works; and when ye remember their works ye may know how that it is said, and also written, that they were good" (Hel. 5:6).

The most notable Book of Mormon admonition to "remember" made reference to the good qualities of the greatest person to ever live on this earth—the Son of God. It is the frequently repeated petition embodied in the sacramental prayers: "that they may eat [or drink] in remembrance . . . and always remember him" (Moro. 4:3; 5:2). The message is clear—feelings and emotions can be created or modified by reflections.

To assist with the process of recalling the good things of the good people we have known, the Holy Spirit extends His influence as a strengthening power while duplicating for us the pattern provided in the Lord's promise: "But the Comforter, which is the Holy Ghost, whom the Father will send in my name, he shall teach you all things, and *bring all things to your remembrance,* whatsoever I have said unto you" (John 14:26; emphasis added). Reaffirming that concept, Elder Neal A. Maxwell taught, "Very importantly, the Holy Ghost brings needed things to our remembrance, so we should prepare by 'treasuring up' precious things in our individual storehouses of memory. All of this can come 'into [our] hearts, . . . in the very hour, yea, in the very moment' (D&C 100:5–6)" (*Moving in His Majesty and Power,* 65).

When friends and loved ones are gone, we are left with our memories of them and their influence upon us. Nothing can be done to create additional memories after mortal life ends; we are left to ponder whatever associations and experiences we shared preceding death. As we grow older, death claims, with an increasing frequency, members of family and circles of close friends. Those of us who remain speak often of what life was like when others were still here. Burdens of absence are lifted as we enjoy reminiscing about our moments together, regardless of how brief or insignificant they may have seemed at the time. Memory cells have a way of recalling some trivial incidents that didn't seem worth remembering—until the person is gone.

Many years ago I visited the boyhood home of President David O. McKay in Huntsville, Utah. In an upstairs hallway was a framed picture of two little girls, older sisters of President McKay, who died at the ages of ten and eleven. Above the pictures is inscribed: "Gone, But Not Forgotten." Absence can make the heart grow fonder, but absence without shared memories of previous associations makes the heart sadder.

Parents gain a perspective of the value of memories when children leave home. As each child has gone away, I have spent a lot of time visiting my memory bank. Always I have wished there had been more deposits, creating a bigger treasury. If memory-making doesn't happen before loved ones leave, nothing can be done to compensate.

We are fortunate if we have shared our lives and spent time with those we will miss most. A grieving soul can be soothed with comforting memories. Elder Neal A. Maxwell observed: "Some memories are exclusive and personal . . . [and] are especially able to move us, to brace us, and to caress us. . . . The quiet massage of memories brings personal refreshment and renewal. After all, in gospel grammar, death is not an exclamation point, merely a comma" (*Moving in His Majesty and Power*, 81, 91).

EXPECTATIONS

An even more sure solace in the face of death revolves around our expectations. Alma asks, "Do you look forward with an eye of faith?" (Alma 5:15). More fortunate are those with warm memories when death comes who also have expectations for the future, based upon a correct understanding of the teachings of the Lord about the answer to Job's question, "If a man die, shall he live again?" (Job 14:14). It is comforting to know that all mortal beings were first born as spirit children of eternal parents and lived in a premortal world of spirits. Then came mortal birth on this earth, when each spirit personage was clothed in a physical body of flesh and blood. The spirit being continues to live in that body throughout mortality until the event we call death, which is the separation of the spirit from its mortal tabernacle. The body dies and decays, but the spirit person does not; he only relocates to another sphere. Alma declared "the soul could never die" (Alma 42:9). Henry Wadsworth Longfellow said the same thing poetically:

Tell me not, in mournful numbers,

Life is but an empty dream!—

For the soul is dead that slumbers,

And things are not what they seem.

Life is real! Life is earnest!

And the grave is not its goal;

Dust thou art, to dust returnest,

Was not spoken of the soul.

(*101 Famous Poems,* 123)

A good friend shared with me the experience of an older neighbor lady whose husband passed away and left her alone, having never had children. She had no siblings and few friends. She was not a Latter-day Saint, though she lived in the midst of many of them. When her husband died, she was angry with the Lord, upon whom she placed the blame for causing her so much loneliness and intense emotional pain. She had no concept of a life hereafter and felt that her husband had ceased to exist. Such ideas left her with feelings of frustration and fear, not knowing what to expect as she looked forward to her own demise and extinction. She came in desperation to my friend, bitterly denouncing a God who had created people with desires to find and feel love for companions, but who are ultimately separated in death without hope thereafter for either spouse or self. He shared with her insights from the doctrines taught by prophets of this and former dispensations. But she could not accept the idea of prophets on earth who communed with a God, and so rejected the very teachings of truth that would have given her comfort.

Without accurate insights, it is difficult to have meaningful expectations concerning a postmortal life; there is a lack of hope for a continuation of associations with loved ones. Even if people possess fond memories from relationships in former days, devilish despair develops in them if they have no anticipation of further contacts.

Prophets have provided a number of insights about the habitation of departed spirits. Listen to the declarations of some of the Lord's spokesmen. President Brigham Young taught: "When you lay down this tabernacle, where are you going? Into the spirit world. Where is the spirit world? It is right here. Do they go beyond the boundaries of this organized earth? No, they do not" (JD, 3:369). The Prophet Joseph Smith saw that "The spirits of the just are exalted to a greater and more glorious work; hence they are blessed in their departure to the world of spirits . . . they are not far from us, and know and understand our thoughts, feelings, and motions, and are often pained therewith" (*TPJS,* 326).

Alma points out that "the spirits of all men, as soon as they are departed from this mortal body, yea, the spirits of all men, whether they be good or evil, are taken home to that God who gave them life" (Alma 40:11). Elder Orson Pratt clarifies the condition of our state immediately after death: "To go back then, into the presence of God, is to be placed in a condition wherein his presence can be seen. It does not mean, in all cases, that people who return into his presence are immediately placed within a few yards or rods or within a short distance of his person" (*JD,* 16:365). President Heber C. Kimball corroborates Elder Pratt's perspective: "As for my going into the immediate presence of God when I die, I do not expect it, but I expect to go into the world of spirits and associate with my brethren, and preach the Gospel in the spiritual world, and prepare myself in every necessary way to receive my body again" (*JD,* 3:112).

Other prophets further clarify conditions in the postmortal world so we can have more focused hopes of the hereafter. Several speak of two general divisions or conditions in the world of spirits: paradise and spirit prison. Alma says that "the spirits of those who are righteous are received into a state of happiness, which is called paradise, a state of rest, a state of peace, where they shall rest from all their troubles and from all care, and sorrow" (Alma 40:12). The Lord, through Joseph Smith, specifies who those righteous are: "For whoso cometh not unto me [by repentance and baptism] is under the bondage of sin. . . . And by this you may know the righteous from the wicked" (D&C 84:51, 53). The righteous, then, are those who have made and kept covenants in the church and Kingdom of God. They are celestial spirits living in paradise who will eventually be resurrected into the celestial kingdom (see D&C 76:50–70).

President Joseph Fielding Smith reaffirmed the identity of the righteous dead in paradise:

> The righteous, those who have kept the commandments of the Lord . . . are in happiness in paradise. They cease from all this trouble, and trial, and tribulation, and anguish of soul. They are free from all these torments, because they have been true and faithful to their covenants. . . . All spirits of men after death return to the spirit world. There, as I understand it, *the righteous—meaning those who have been baptized and who have been faithful*—are gathered in one part and all the others in another part of the spirit world (*Doctrines of Salvation,* 2:230; emphasis added).

Some people have been confused by misunderstanding a statement attributed to the Savior. It is recorded that while He was hanging on the cross, Jesus spoke to the thief in these words: "Today shalt thou be with me in paradise" (Luke 23:43). Is it possible for an unrighteous thief to become worthy in an instant to occupy a place where covenant-keeping people reside in the presence of the Savior? The Prophet Joseph Smith clarified this apparent inconsistency with the following explanation: "King James' translators make it out to say paradise. But what is paradise? It is a modern word: it does not answer at all to the original word that Jesus made use of. . . . There is nothing in the original word in Greek from which this was taken that signifies paradise; but it was—This day thou shalt be with me in the world of spirits" (*TPJS,* 309).

The other major condition of postmortal spirits is spirit prison. Clearly anyone bound over to an existence in prison is not free. The Savior taught how all can avoid bondage: "If ye continue in my word, then are ye my disciples indeed; And ye shall know the truth, and the truth shall make you free" (John 8:31–32). We know, then, that those spirits who are consigned to spirit prison are without the blessings and covenants of the gospel. Either they have never been taught the gospel, or they rejected it, or they may have received it and then failed to abide by what they were taught.

This group is made up of at least two general classes. The first consists of honorable people who live good lives by being generous and honest in their dealings with their fellowmen. They include God-fearing people who worship according to their understanding. They are terrestrial spirits who are presently worthy of an eventual inheritance in the terrestrial kingdom. (See D&C 76:71–80.) There may be many of these who have not had the gospel presented to them in mortality, but who accept it when they are taught in the spirit world. When the vicarious priesthood ordinances are performed for them in earthly temples, they are provided with a valid claim upon a celestial inheritance in the kingdom of our Father, thus breaking the bands of spiritual bondage.

The others in spirit prison are wicked people characterized as liars, sorcerers, adulterers, and murderers. This group not only experiences the absence of gospel blessings, but also suffers for previously committed evil deeds for which no repentance has taken place. These are telestial spirits who await the second resurrection and an inheritance in the glory of the telestial kingdom. (See D&C 76:89, 101, 103, 106, 112; Revelation 21:8.) There are also in this spirit prison sons of perdition, those who deny and defy the power of God. They will be resurrected, but then will be cast out permanently into outer darkness, a kingdom without glory. (See D&C 76:30–49.)

Prophets not only provide descriptions of postmortal life; they also provide insights into what we will do there. President Joseph F.

Smith saw a vision of the redemption of the dead in which he learned that when the Savior visited the spirit world following His own death, "he organized his forces and appointed messengers, clothed with power and authority, and commissioned them to go forth and carry the light of the gospel to them that were in darkness, even to all the spirits of men; and thus was the gospel preached to the dead" (D&C 138:30). This was the beginning of the teaching of the gospel to those in the spirit world who were not yet enjoying the privileges of the Lord's covenant people. Who are those messengers? President Smith continued in describing his vision: "I beheld that the faithful elders of this dispensation, when they depart from mortal life, continue their labors in the preaching of the gospel of repentance and redemption, through the sacrifice of the Only Begotten Son of God, among those who are in darkness and under the bondage of sin in the great world of the spirits of the dead" (D&C 138:57). If we knew all that is being done in that spirit world, we would likely discover right-eous men and women who have completed their mortal existence and who are engaged in many familiar tasks. Likely, the Church orga-nization and duties of its members there will not be strange to those who have rendered faithful service here.

Speaking at a funeral service, President Heber J. Grant told of an illuminating experience concerning the spirit world activity of Fera Young following his death in young manhood:

One of my nearest and dearest friends in boyhood was Horace G. Whitney. Horace had a dream after Fera died in which the two had a conversation. Horace asked him what he was doing and received this reply: "I am here working, Horace, with the wayward boys and girls of the Church who are drifting away from it, and I am trying to turn their hearts back to the truth. That is my calling and it is of far greater importance than it would have been for me to remain upon the earth. I have a great influence with them" (*Improvement Era*, Feb. 1931).

President Brigham Young described the engagement of deceased faithful Saints in teaching activities for the benefit of those who need to hear the message of the gospel:

He [Joseph Smith] has just as much labor on hand as I have; he has just as much to do. Father Smith and Carlos and brother Partridge, yes, and every other good Saint, are just as busy in the spirit world as you and I are here. They can see us, but we cannot see them unless our eyes were opened. What are they doing there? They are preaching, preaching all the time, and preparing the way for us to hasten our work in building temples here and elsewhere. . . . When the faithful Elders, holding this Priesthood, go into the spirit world they carry with them the same power and Priesthood that they had while in the mortal tabernacle. They have got the victory over the power of the enemy here, consequently when they leave this world they have perfect control over those evil spirits, and they cannot be buffeted by Satan (*JD*, 3:370–71).

Many among us wonder about the conditions of postmortality even more than about what we will be doing there. What will it feel like after we die? Prophets also provide perspective on life in the spirit world. Brigham Young visualized what his life might be like in the spirit world, describing it as though it had already happened:

I have passed from a state of sorrow, grief, mourning, woe, misery, pain, anguish and disappointment into a state of existence, where I can enjoy life to the fullest extent as far as that can be done without a body. My spirit is set free, I thirst no more, I want to sleep no more, I hunger no more, I tire no more, I run, I walk, I labor, I go, I come, I do this, I do that, whatever is required of me, nothing like pain or weariness. I am full of life, full of vigor, and I enjoy the presence of my Heavenly Father, by the power of his Spirit (*JD*, 17:142).

An inspired statement made by Joseph Smith will shed some light on the conditions of individuals and our relationships with each other: "And that same sociality which exists among us here will exist among us there, only it will be coupled with eternal glory, which glory we do not now enjoy" (D&C 130:2).

President Joseph F. Smith expands that insight on our life hereafter:

What a glorious thought it is, to me at least, and it must be to all who have conceived of the truth or received it in their hearts, that those from whom we have to part here, we will meet again and see as they are. We will meet the same identical being that we associated with here in the flesh—not some other soul, some other being, or the same being in some other form, but the same identity and the same form and likeness, the same person we knew and were associated with in our mortal existence, even to the wounds in the flesh. Not that a person will always be marred by scars, wounds, deformities, defects or infirmities, for these will be removed in their course, in their proper time, according to the merciful providence of God. Deformity will be removed;

defects will be eliminated, and men and women shall attain to the perfection of their spirits, to the perfection that God designed in the beginning (*Gospel Doctrine*, 23).

As to some of the conditions one might expect to find in the celestial kingdom, where resurrected celestial beings will dwell, Elder Orson Pratt provided some insight:

A Saint, who is one in deed and in truth, does not look for an immaterial heaven but he expects a heaven with lands, houses, cities, vegetation, rivers, and animals; with thrones, temples, palaces, kings, princes, priests, and angels; with food, raiment, musical instruments, etc.; all of which are material. Indeed the Saints' heaven is a redeemed, glorified, celestial material creation, inhabited by glorified material beings, male and female, organized into families, embracing all the relationships of husbands and wives, parents and children, where sorrow, crying, pain, and death will be known no more. Or to speak still more definitely, this earth, when glorified, is the Saints' eternal heaven (*Millennial Star*, Vol. 28, 722, Nov. 17, 1866).

No one fails to experience four of the inherited results of the Fall of Adam, all of which contain blessed opportunities for Adam's posterity:

First is the privilege of being born into mortality and receiving a body. With that privilege comes the responsibility to recognize and choose to live by values that provide lasting and joyful results, or face the consequences of alternative choices. (See Moses 5:11.)

The Fall also introduced an escape from the hazards, sorrows, trials, and tribulations that accompany this mortal existence. No one wants to live in mortal conditions forever. Jacob taught that "death hath passed upon all men, to fulfill the merciful plan of the great Creator" (2 Ne. 9:6).

Because of the Fall, all mankind experience a spiritual death, meaning they are cut off from the presence of God. However, every mortal will also remain in His presence forever, whereas the wicked will experience a second spiritual death when they are judged unworthy to remain with Him. (See Hel. 14:15–18.)

Another result of the Fall, as taught by Jacob, is that "the resurrection must needs come unto man by reason of the fall" (2 Ne. 9:6). Those spirits who have lost their bodies through death consider themselves to be in bondage, though not forever. (See D&C 45:17.) The Apostle Paul wrote, "For as in Adam all die, even so in Christ shall all be made alive" (1 Cor. 15:22). That power of resurrection that comes from on high, according to Lehi, is "the power of the Spirit" (2 Ne. 2:8). The promise of a resurrection of the body provides relief to those who grieve over the loss of loved ones.

An additional consolation we find in the prophetic insights on death is the promise of comfort and peace. Sincere and caring friends commonly extend expressions of comfort. Friends often provide meals and lodging, while others voluntarily bear logistical, financial, or other types of burdens in behalf of those who grieve. The very presence of someone who understands is a source of solace.

But even under the best of circumstances, the ability to touch the tender feelings of a grieving soul with comforting, penetrating relief and to replace anguish with internal peace is not a power delegated to mortal beings. Those who sincerely look to the Lord for His love at times of bereavement can come to understand why the Holy Ghost is called a Comforter. The Holy Spirit soothing our spirit is the ultimate source of peace (see Gal. 5:22). It is truly a power from on high. President Heber J. Grant shared an intimate moment in the life of his family that portrayed the capacity of the Lord to adjust and modify feelings at the time of death of a loved one. Near the time of his wife's passing, he gathered his children to say their farewells. His twelve-year-old daughter begged her father to give her mama a healing priesthood blessing. President Grant felt strongly that it was his wife's time to go, and instead petitioned the Lord for strength and comfort, both for himself and for his little children. He then relates the following:

> Within an hour my wife passed away, and I called the children back into the room. My little boy about five and a half or six years of age was weeping bitterly, and the little girl twelve years of age took him in her arms and said: "Do not weep, do not cry, Heber; since we went out of this room the voice of the Lord from heaven has said to me, 'In the death of your mamma the will of the Lord shall be done.'"
>
> Tell me, my friends, that I do not know that God hears and answers prayers! Tell me that I do not know that in the hour of adversity the Latter-day Saints are comforted and blessed and consoled as no other people are (*Gospel Standards*, 361).

President Grant provides a prophetic key to accessing heavenly powers to obtain divine peace and be consoled by the God and Father of us all. The prerequisite key that persuaded the young girl to ask her father to bless her mother and that inspired President Grant to plead with the Lord for a blessing in behalf of his children was faith in the Lord Jesus Christ. Both the daddy and daughter possessed faith in the existence and powers of God that made possible the extension of the heavenly influence.

President Harold B. Lee also identifies the key to obtaining heavenly consolation:

> Heaven is not far removed from him who in deep sorrow looks confidently forward to the glorious day of resurrection. . . .
>
> So to you who have lost loved ones, to you who know the pangs of loneliness, some of us have also gone through the fire and understand what it means. We say to you that in the faith that lifts you beyond the sordid trials of the day and points you to the glorious tomorrow that can be yours if you too, like the prophet Job, can say, "I know that my redeemer lives."
>
> I leave you my blessing, to bring you the peace that can come only from this knowledge and from the witness that you can receive if you will put your trust in your heavenly Father (*From the Valley of Despair to the Mountain Peaks of Hope,* 12–13).

Death ultimately comes to everyone, and is accompanied by grief. But, like the soothing strains of soft music created by talented fingers on harp strings, comfort is found in the satisfying influences of warm memories. Settled feelings of peace replace anxious fears and doubts when our expectations of life after death are couched in faith in the prophetic truths of the gospel of Jesus Christ. We welcome the resultant power from on high as the Holy Spirit pervades and prevails in our hearts and homes; it sustains and strengthens us in the aftermath of death.

As we humbly celebrate the redeeming Atonement of the Savior, we are reminded of a prayer, often sung by choirs, in which St. Francis of Assisi declared, "It is in dying that we are born to eternal life" (*Prayer of St. Francis of Assisi*). Only in the Atonement of Christ does power come from on high to transfer sin to the Savior or to transport righteous earthbound souls to the paradisiacal world of righteous spirits and from thence to a resurrected and exalted state of immortality and eternal life. Those who exercise faith in Him "have hope through the atonement of Christ and the *power of his resurrection,* to be raised unto life eternal, and this because of your faith in him according to the promise" (Moro. 7:41; emphasis added).

CHAPTER 14
THE POWER OF REDEMPTION
FOR LITTLE CHILDREN WHO DIE

In the last chapter, we talked about the power of the Spirit that comes to us from prophetic insights on the subject of death. This chapter deals with a specific segment of our people, namely children, whose deaths raise some questions that are unique to that group. Scriptural passages and recorded statements from the prophetic authorities of the Church provide some answers that are both informational and inspirational. Since heavenly channels provide the means by which these truths are revealed, the ensuing spiritual power, whether in the form of increased understanding or peace and spiritual comfort, obviously comes from on high.

On June 6, 1954, I had been serving as a missionary for six months. My missionary service had an unusual dimension to it—I was married. During the Korean War a limited number of young married men were called as missionaries, and I had the privilege of serving when it had previously appeared that I would not be able to. My wife was expecting our first child and, though we were separated geographically, we were unitedly and anxiously looking forward to June. When the phone rang one Sunday evening in our missionary apartment, I knew it could be the call. But the "Hello, son" from my father carried an ominous tone, and I knew something was wrong. He explained that our newborn son had arrived, but only after a very difficult delivery. My wife was fine and the baby was alive, but in critical condition. He would inform me of future developments.

The next few hours provided an unusual emotional conflict. Each hour of not knowing intensified the fear that conditions were worsening at home. But not hearing also increased my hope that the situation was improving and everything would eventually be all right. I wasn't sure I wanted to know more. The next phone call terminated that conflict—our son had passed away after a mortal life of only ten hours.

After the first emotional shock waves subsided, I sought for answers. Mostly I framed a lot of questions. What will happen to our son? What will his future be? Why did he have to die? My missionary companion, Elder Keith Perkins, patiently listened through it all and sincerely sought to help me find strength to carry my sorrow. I treasure the memory of him tenderly nurturing me and lovingly sharing my grief. We talked for hours about gospel principles pertaining to purposes of life and death; the weight of my burdens was literally lightened by an unseen spiritual power from on high.

Though I hadn't time or resources then, I determined that one day I would search the doctrines of the Church and learn the status and destiny of little children who die. Some years later, when my wife and I experienced a pregnancy that ended in a miscarriage, I determined that the time had arrived to find what information I could on this subject. I remembered the comfort the Holy Spirit had provided me while learning some of the things the Lord and His servants had said on this vital subject, and I wanted others to have access to the same information.

Since there is a difference between what has been said concerning children who have drawn the breath of life in mortality and those who are described as stillborn, we should discuss them separately.

CHILDREN WHO DIE BEFORE THE AGE OF ACCOUNTABILITY

What about infants who die? Do they need baptism, an ordinance of the priesthood universally required for salvation? The need for it could be inferred from some scriptural statements: "Except a man be born of water and of the Spirit, he cannot enter into the kingdom of God" (John 3:5). "He that believeth and is baptized shall be saved; but he that believeth not shall be damned" (Mark 16:16).

From other passages, however, it is evident that statements declaring the necessity of baptism refer only to those who have arrived at an age and condition of accountability before the Lord:

Little children are redeemed from the foundation of the world through mine Only Begotten;

Wherefore, they cannot sin, for power is not given unto Satan to tempt little children, until they begin to become accountable before me (D&C 29:46–47).

For all men must repent and be baptized, and not only men, but women, and children who have arrived at the years of accountability (D&C 18:42).

Children shall be baptized for the remission of their sins when eight years old, and receive the laying on of the hands (D&C 68:27).

Little children need no repentance, neither baptism. . . . But little children are alive in Christ. . . . He that supposeth that little children need baptism is in the gall of bitterness and in the bonds of iniquity; for he hath neither faith, hope, nor charity (Moro. 8:11–12, 14).

This last passage cited is not only an injunction against the practice of infant baptism, but also provides a description of the despair experienced by some parents who lose unbaptized children in death and lack understanding of the doctrine of Christ on the subject.

Brigham Young was once asked, "Should children who die before they attain the age of eight years be baptized for, or receive any temple ordinances, other than being sealed to their parents?" His answer: "Nothing more than to be sealed to their parents" (*John Nuttall Journal*).

Since baptism is not required for little children, what is their status in the next life? In a vision received in the Kirtland Temple the Prophet Joseph Smith was permitted to behold the celestial kingdom of God, after which he shared a definitive doctrinal insight: "And I also beheld that all children who die before they arrive at the years of accountability are saved in the celestial kingdom of heaven" (D&C 137:10).

There are authoritative assurances that to be "saved in the celestial kingdom" means receiving all of the blessings of exaltation for children who die before reaching accountability:

And little children also have eternal life [exaltation] (Mosiah 15:5).

The Lord will grant unto these children the privilege of all the sealing blessings which pertain to the exaltation. . . . It would be manifestly unfair to deprive a little child of the privilege of receiving all the blessings of exaltation in the world to come simply because it died in infancy (*Doctrines of Salvation*, 2:54).

I lost a son six years of age and I saw him a man in the spirit world after his death, and I saw how he had exercised his own freedom of choice and would obtain of his own will and volition a companionship, and in due time to him and all those who are worthy of it, shall come all of the blessings and sealing privileges of the house of the Lord (Melvin J. Ballard, *The Three Degrees of Glory*, 34).

But, with little children who are taken away in infancy and innocence before they have reached the years of accountability, and are not capable of committing sin, the gospel reveals to us the fact that they are redeemed, and Satan has no power over them. . . . Such children are in the bosom of the Father. They will inherit their glory and their exaltation, and they will not be deprived of the blessings that belong to them; . . . and in the wisdom and mercy and economy of God our Heavenly Father, all that could have been obtained and enjoyed by them if they had been permitted to live in the flesh will be provided for them hereafter. They will lose nothing by being taken away from us in this way (*Gospel Doctrine*, 452–53).

On Sunday, March 20, 1842, the Prophet Joseph Smith spoke at a funeral service for a deceased child. During the course of his remarks he provided a comforting insight: "The Lord takes many away, even in infancy, that they may escape the envy of man, and the sorrows and evils of this present world; they were too pure, too lovely, to live on earth; therefore, if rightly considered, instead of mourning we have reason to rejoice as they are delivered from evil, and we shall soon have them again" (*HC*, 4:553).

In support of this teaching of Joseph Smith, Elder Bruce R. McConkie said that his father-in-law, President Joseph Fielding Smith, told him one time that "we must assume that the Lord knows and arranges beforehand who shall be taken in infancy and who shall remain on earth to undergo whatever tests are needed in their cases" ("The Salvation of Little Children," *Ensign*, Apr. 1977, 6).

The Prophet Joseph's assurance that "we shall soon have them again" is borne out by the following narrative of Sister M. Isabella Horne:

> In conversation with the Prophet Joseph Smith once in Nauvoo, the subject of children in the resurrection was broached. I believe it was in Sister Leonora Cannon Taylor's house. She had just lost one of her children, and I had also lost one previously. The Prophet wanted to comfort us, and he told us that we should receive those children in the morning of the resurrection just as we laid them down, in purity and innocence, and we should nourish and care for them as their mothers. He said that children would be raised in the resurrection just as they were laid down, and that they would obtain all the intelligence necessary to occupy thrones, principalities and powers. . . . The children would grow and develop in the Millennium, and that the mothers would have the pleasure of training and caring for them, which they had been deprived of in this life (*HC*, 4:556, footnote).

In an editorial on the Resurrection in the June 1904 *Improvement Era*, President Joseph F. Smith said:

The body will come forth as it is laid to rest, for there is no growth or development in the grave. As it is laid down, so will it arise, and changes to perfection will come by the law of restitution. But the spirit will continue to expand and develop, and the body, after the resurrection will develop to the full stature of man.

This may be accepted as the doctrine of the Church in respect to the resurrection of children and their future development to the full stature of men and women; and it is alike conformable to that which will be regarded as both reasonable and desirable (*HC,* 4:557).

As to the physical stature and appearance of the spirit of a child who dies, we are informed by President Joseph F. Smith:

The spirits of our children are immortal before they come to us, and their spirits, after bodily death, are like they were before they came. They are as they would have appeared if they had lived in the flesh, to grow to maturity, or to develop their physical bodies to the full stature of their spirits. If you see one of your children that has passed away it may appear to you in the form in which you would recognize it, the form of childhood; but if it came to you as a messenger bearing some important truth, it would perhaps come . . . in the stature of full-grown manhood, . . . our children were full-grown and possessed their full stature in the spirit, before they entered mortality, the same stature that they will possess after they have passed away from mortality, and as they will also appear after the resurrection, when they shall have completed their mission. . . . There is restitution, there is growth, there is development, after the resurrection from death (*Gospel Doctrine,* 455–56).

Six commonly asked questions pertaining to the status of children who die were answered by Elder Bruce R. McConkie:

1. Are all little children saved automatically in the celestial kingdom?

    To this question the answer is a thunderous *yes.* . . . If it were not so the redemption would not be infinite in its application.

2. Will children have eternal life?

    We have quoted scriptures saying that children will be saved in the celestial kingdom, but now face the further query as to whether this includes the greatest of all the gifts of God—the gift of eternal life. And in the providences of Him who is infinitely wise, the answer is in the affirmative. Salvation means eternal life; the two terms are synonymous; they mean exactly the same thing.

3. Will children be married and live in the family unit?

    Certainly. There can be no question about this. If they gain salvation, which is eternal life, which is exaltation, it means that they are married and live in the family unit.

4. Will children ever be tested?

    Absolutely not! Any idea that they will be tested in paradise or during the millennium or after the millennium is pure fantasy. Why would a resurrected being, who has already come forth from the grave with a celestial body and whose salvation is guaranteed, be tested? Would the Lord test someone who cannot fail the test and whose exaltation is guaranteed? "Satan cannot tempt little children in this life, nor in the spirit world, nor after their resurrection. Little children who die before reaching the years of accountability will not be tempted" (*Doctrines of Salvation*, 56–57).

5. What is the age of accountability?

Accountability does not burst full-bloom upon a child at any given moment in his life. Children become accountable gradually, over a number of years. Becoming accountable is a process, not a goal to be attained when a specified number of years, days, and hours have elapsed. In our revelation the Lord says, "They cannot sin, for power is not given unto Satan to tempt little children, until they begin to become accountable before me" (D&C 29:47). There comes a time, however, when accountability is real and actual, and sin is attributed in the lives of those who develop normally. It is eight years of age, the age of baptism. (See D&C 68:27.)

6. What about the mentally deficient?

It is with them as it is with little children. They never arrive at the years of accountability and are considered as though they were little children. . . . They need no baptism; they are alive in Christ; and they will receive, inherit, and possess in eternity on the same basis as do all children. After revealing that little children are redeemed . . . the Lord applied the same principles to those who are mentally deficient. "And again, I say unto you, that whoso having knowledge, have I not

commanded to repent? And he that hath no understanding, it remaineth in me to do according as it is
written" (D&C 29:49–50). ("The Salvation of Little
Children," *Ensign*, Apr. 1977, 6–7)

So we see that whenever a child of any race or nationality dies
in infancy before the age of accountability, provision has been
made for it to be exalted in the celestial kingdom of God through
the power of the redeeming sacrifice of the Savior. Worthy parents,
to whom the child has been sealed, will receive these children unto
themselves in the First Resurrection and rear them during their
growth processes to the full stature of adulthood. All ordinances
that are necessary for their exaltation will likely be performed for
them in the temples during the millennium.

STILLBORN CHILDREN

Before discussing the status of children who are born without life
in the body, it is important to reaffirm a basic principle. Whenever
life exists, there will eventually be both a death and a resurrection
of that entity. Paul taught the Corinthians, "For as in Adam all die,
even so in Christ shall all be made alive" (1 Cor. 15:22). So our
discussion will be concerned with whether life existed in the case of
a stillborn child. If the body has actually housed a spirit, the child
will be resurrected and an heir to the exalting blessings discussed
earlier. But if the spirit does not enter the body, there can be no
resurrection.

Mortality begins when the spirit is united with the physical
body, thus creating a living soul. (See D&C 88:15.) The critical
question is, "When does the uniting of the spirit and body take
place?" In an informal survey, I submitted this question to 216
high school seminary juniors and seniors who expressed the

following opinions:

a. At conception   23%

b. At birth   40%

c. After conception, but prior to birth   37%

Such a divergence of opinion may not be indicative of the understanding of the general Church membership, but the survey may well represent a general lack of consensus among the members of the Church on a very vital unanswered question. The reason for the lack of clarity and clear understanding is simple—authorities of the Church have not made a doctrinal declaration or defined an official Church teaching on the subject. However, various opinions have been expressed by several whose thinking is highly respected, and these merit serious consideration. For the present, individuals are free to consider alternative explanations and seek confirmation by the Spirit of that which is true and appropriate for them to believe. Some significant statements have been expressed in response to each of the suggested answers to the question, "When might the spirit enter the body?"

At Conception

Nothing has been found containing any statements of Church authorities in support of this idea. A few have privately disavowed the possibility. This concept is taught by the Catholic Church, whose doctrine does not allow for a premortal existence of the spirit, but teaches instead that the beginning of life for both the body and the spirit is at the time of conception. They feel that "original sin attaches at the moment of conception . . . and in the event of an abortion or miscarriage, the fetus or blood clot must be baptized" (*Mormon Doctrine*, 347). They require baptism for unborn children to save them since they believe the child to have been alive from conception. If one assumes the possibility that a fully developed spirit child of God would or could inhabit an unformed, undeveloped, embryonic mass, then what would happen if the mother loses the substance in the first few months of pregnancy? The conclusion must be that a resurrection would occur for the mass or substance as it appeared at the time of such loss—a foolish notion.

At Birth

In December 1953 a well-known brother gave a talk in Salt Lake. I vividly recall that he dramatically declared his opinion that the spirit enters the body of the child when the baby emerges from the mother's womb. He suggested that no one knows the precise moment of that occurrence, but it is part of the birth process, not before. Others share this opinion. A passage recorded in 3 Nephi is often cited in support of this belief:

> And it came to pass that he [Nephi] cried mightily unto the Lord all that day; and behold, the voice of the Lord came unto him, saying:
> Lift up your head and be of good cheer; for behold, the time is at hand, and on this night shall the sign be given, and on the morrow come I into the world, to show unto the world that I will fulfil all that which I have caused to be spoken by the mouth of my holy prophets (3 Ne. 1:12–13).

Two assumptions are often connected with this scriptural statement. First, it is assumed that the spirit of the Savior had not yet inhabited the unborn fetus which was being prepared for birth by His mother because Nephi heard the voice of Jesus on the American continent on the eve of His birth in Bethlehem. The second assumption is that Jesus can be viewed as a prototype for the human race, and all mankind will pursue the same course that He followed. Those assumptions lead to the conclusion that the baby's spirit enters the body at birth rather than before.

The first justification may very well be valid. It is not, however, without question. In this day of communication technology, it is not difficult to imagine a transmission of sound halfway around the world. Surely the Lord could have caused such a happening two thousand years ago. There is no evidence that the Savior was personally present on the American continent when he spoke to Nephi. It is also possible that a heavenly messenger was designated as a spokesman and invested with divine authority to speak to Nephi on behalf of Jesus.

Such investiture of divine authority is not without precedent on other occasions, such as the time Joseph Smith set out to procure wine for a sacrament meeting and was "met by a heavenly messenger" (*HC*, 1:106). The first words spoken by that messenger representing the Lord were: "Listen to the voice of Jesus Christ, your Lord, your God, and your Redeemer" (D&C 27:1). It is not impossible that the spirit of the Savior did occupy His body prior to birth and yet a voice could still have been heard by Nephi thousands of miles distant.

The second justification, the assumption that all people follow the patterns set by the Savior, is even more problematic. Even if Jesus did not enter His physical body until His birth, there is no conclusive evidence that the rest of mankind do not inhabit their respective bodies before birth. There are many phases of the Savior's sojourn upon this earth that are "exceptions to the rule" as far as our lives are concerned. His mother conceived Him in an "exceptional" manner. His life without sin was also without precedent. His power over life and death has not been possessed by any other. His life as a God before mortality and as a God in a mortal body has never been duplicated. His knowledge of all things and His infinite ability to know and fulfill the will of His Father is worthy of emulation but has never been matched by mortals. His power to resurrect His body was a "first" for earth's inhabitants. It is not only possible, but likely, that He did many other things differently, including His pre-birth activities. It is possible that the spirit enters the body at the time of birth, but that is certainly not an inevitable conclusion.

After Conception but Prior to Birth

The unborn fetus does not have to wait the full nine months of pregnancy before all organs and functional component systems of the body are developed. Many children who are born prior to full term are healthy and normal in every respect. A pediatrician in Salt Lake City once told me that in rare instances babies have been born as early as five months after conception and lived without permanent disabilities. It is possible that a spirit could inhabit a fully developed body some length of time before birth.

President J. Reuben Clark proposed the interesting conjecture that while in our premortal state, we may have participated in an educational process of learning how to operate and manipulate a complicated physical body before we actually came to live on earth in a mortal tabernacle. (See *Man—God's Greatest Miracle*, 31.) If so, might that educational process include the spirit entering the body some time before birth in order to actually experience operating and controlling the body with all of its organic parts and systems prior to beginning a life in mortality?

Some time after the body is formed and prepared to receive it, the spirit enters its mortal tabernacle and becomes a living soul.

(See Moses 3:7; Abr. 5:7.) In a discourse delivered at a funeral service July 19, 1874, Brigham Young suggested a time when the spirit enters the body:

> When the mother feels life come to her infant it is the spirit entering the body preparatory to the immortal existence. But suppose an accident occurs and the spirit has to leave this body prematurely, what then? All that the physician says is—"it is a still birth," and that is all they know about it; but whether the spirit remains in the body a minute, an hour, a day, a year, or lives there until the body has reached a good old age, it is certain that the time will come when they will be separated, and the body will return to mother earth. . . . We have bodies which . . . will be prepared to come forth in the glorious resurrection (*JD,* 17:143–44).

The time when the spirit enters the body is referred to as the "time of quickening" in a statement made by the First Presidency, Joseph F. Smith, John R. Winder, and Anthon H. Lund: "True it is that the body of man enters upon its career as a tiny germ or embryo, which becomes an infant, quickened at a certain stage by the spirit whose tabernacle it is, and the child, after being born, develops into a man" (*Improvement Era,* Nov. 1909, 80).

President J. Reuben Clark made an additional comment on this subject when discussing the passage recorded in Abraham 5:7:

> We note this account of Abraham apparently deals with the body after its formation, and gives the account of its advent into the world as a living, breathing body. We also note that seemingly the spirit enters the body before the world-life spoken of comes. . . . It seems possible that the spirit may

not be present in the embryo till at least shortly before birth, whether the birth be regular or premature. . . . Yet every mother testifies there is life in the embryo months before birth, for she feels it (*Man—God's Greatest Miracle*, 19–20).

President Joseph Fielding Smith observed:

There is no information given by revelation in regard to the status of stillborn children. However, I will express my personal opinion that we should have hope that *these little ones will receive a resurrection and then belong to us.* I cannot help feeling that this will be the case.

When a couple has a stillborn child, we give them all the comfort we can. We have good reasons to hope. Funeral services may be held for such children, if the parents so desire. . . . It is suggested that parents record in their own family records a name for each such stillborn child (*Doctrines of Salvation*, 2:280; emphasis added).

There is an interesting suggestion in scripture that allows for the spirit to enter the body prior to the actual birth of the body: "Inasmuch as ye were born into the world by water, and blood, and the spirit, which I have made, and so became of dust a living soul" (Moses 6:59). There are three elements involved in the creation of a living soul: water, blood, and spirit. The unborn fetus is surrounded in a protective enclosure of water. Nourishment comes through the blood. The body is then "quickened" by the spirit, and the infant is prepared to be born "into the world." Perhaps this concept of a living entity existing before birth explains the actions of the unborn child of Elizabeth when the mother of the Son of God came to visit: "And Mary arose in those days, and went into the hill country with haste, into a city of Judah;

"And entered into the house of Zacharias, and saluted Elisabeth. . . .

"When Elisabeth heard the salutation of Mary, the babe leaped in her womb; . . .

"And she [Elisabeth] spake out . . .

"As soon as the voice of thy salutation sounded in mine ears, the babe leaped in my womb for joy" (Luke 1:39–42, 44). Was the unborn John the Baptist sensitive to the presence of the noble mother of an unborn God?

Parents of some stillborn children may have reason for hope. If the bodies of those children reached a sufficiently developed stage during pregnancy that they were quickened by the spirit, there must have been a "living soul." We place our confidence and faith in the Lord's declaration that "the spirit and the body are the soul of man. And the resurrection from the dead is the redemption of the soul" (D&C 88:15–16).

Infants whose spirits leave their bodies following their occupancy of mortal tabernacles (regardless of the timing of that departure) look forward to the blessings of the Resurrection and being reunited with family members. That reunion is promised to worthy parents who have been recipients of the priesthood sealing powers in the temples of God. The Lord's power of resurrection was not limited to Himself, nor just to parents and adults. Children are also universal recipients of His atoning power that redeems the children who die after becoming living souls, but before they are accountable for actions in mortality.

My wife and I never learned the purposes the Lord may have had in the decision that took our firstborn child. But we were sustained by an understanding of principles of the gospel. Rather than laboring over questions for which we did not receive answers, we gained peace by standing at the wall of faith. We were reassured by the Lord's statement to Joseph Smith and Sidney Rigdon when they were separated from their loved ones: "Your families are well; they are in mine hands, and I will do with them as seemeth me good; for in me there is all power" (D&C 100:1).

We failed to learn why the Lord thought it was "good" for our son to leave us so soon after birth. But we did learn we must trust Him and His judgment. If we seek His wisdom and power in behalf of our family members, we must then also trust His decisions concerning them. We fully expect and have complete confidence that His explanations will one day provide understanding of reasons. Meanwhile, our faith in our Savior has produced hope and confidence, and we have been comforted by power from on high.

CHAPTER 15
POWER IN UNITY

The term *unity* is commonly used in a sociological sense to describe favorable and harmonious conditions among people of a certain culture, organization, or family, etc. Even nations are sometimes described as being united in a common cause.

However, in the Lord's kingdom, conditions of righteous unity are only achieved by following the pattern taught by the Savior as a doctrinal concept that needs to be understood and applied. Scripturally speaking, unity has a spiritual dimension that is the only basis upon which attempts to unify people will succeed. Unity in righteous social structures will likewise endure when founded on the Savior's directives to His people.

The concept is contained in the Savior's great intercessory prayer as recorded in John 17:14–22. The Savior prayed that His disciples and all others who should believe in Him should be one. After quoting that passage, President David O. McKay declared that text to be

> taken from one of the most glorious prayers—I suppose *the greatest prayer—ever uttered in the world,* not excepting the Lord's Prayer. This was Christ's prayer uttered just before he entered the Garden of Gethsemane on the night of his betrayal.

The occasion itself would be impressive to John, and undoubtedly as they knelt there in that upper room before they went through that beautiful gate into Gethsemane, the garden of olives at the base of the Mount of Olives, he noted particularly the plea of the Savior. *I know of no more important chapter in the Bible.* . . . I feel impressed that *there is no more important message to give than to be one* (CR, Oct. 1967, 5; emphasis added).

That prayer is a plea for unity, a prayer for oneness. Of further great interest is a statement made by the Savior eighteen centuries later, on January 2, 1831. Speaking to the Saints in the early days of the Church, He declared, "I say unto you, be one; and if ye are not one ye are not mine" (D&C 38:27). Whereas in 33 A.D. the Savior prayed and pled for unity amongst His people, in our dispensation He is not just pleading; He is directing. He is giving a divine mandate in two words, "Be one."

We may wonder why the heavy emphasis on achieving unity among the Lord's people. Perhaps we should remember His declared objective for His work in this dispensation. He said, "For I will raise up unto myself *a pure people,* that will serve me in righteousness; And all that call upon the name of the Lord, and keep his commandments, shall be saved" (D&C 100:16–17; emphasis added). Just two months earlier, He had said that Zion was the pure in heart (see D&C 97:21). We also note that the Lord revealed on the very day He established His church that His prophet, Joseph Smith, had been "inspired to move the *cause of Zion in mighty power*" (D&C 21:7; emphasis added). So we conclude that the Lord has established His church in order to develop a pure-in-heart people who are united with Him and with each other in a Zion society. There is to be power from on high in the Church and for His people when they achieve conditions of unity.

Such conditions have been achieved before. There was an extended period of peace following the Savior's visit to the Americas during which the people were described in glowing terms as follows:

> The people were all converted unto the Lord, . . . there were no . . . disputations among them, and every man did deal justly one with another. . . .
>
> There was no contention in the land, because of the love of God which did dwell in the hearts of the people.
>
> And there were no envyings, nor strifes, nor tumults, nor [any manner of wickedness]; and surely there could not be a happier people among all the people who had been created by the hand of God. . . .
>
> *They were in one,* the children of Christ, and heirs to the kingdom of God (4 Ne. 1:2, 15–17; emphasis added).

There was power in unity.

We recall that a city of Zion was established under the leadership of the prophet Enoch. The people were also called Zion "because they were of *one heart and one mind,* and dwelt in righteousness" (Moses 7:18; emphasis added). There was power in unity.

In contrast, we note that in the early days of the Church, many Saints immigrated to Missouri with the objective of establishing a Zion place in these latter days. Subsequently, they were driven out of their settlements, and a group of brethren known as Zion's Camp was sent to Missouri to assist with the redemption of Zion. After their arrival in Missouri, the Lord determined that "in

consequence of the transgressions of my people, it is expedient in
me that mine elders should wait for a little season for the redemption of Zion" (D&C 105:9). The Lord described why the people
were unable to establish Zion: "They have not learned to be
obedient to the things which I required at their hands . . . and *are
not united* according to the union required by the law of the celestial kingdom; and Zion cannot be built up unless it is by the principles of the law of the celestial kingdom; otherwise I cannot
receive her unto myself (D&C 105:3–5; emphasis added).

The people lacked the power of unity.

Having learned of the critical need for unity within the Lord's
people, we need to see how that principle is applied and how it can
become an effective influence in our lives. Let me describe that
concept as follows:

Imagine a graphic in which we use two symbols representing
two individuals. Let's assume the two people are a husband and
wife. We will place a solid line between them, representing the
state of unity or harmony that should exist in their marriage. This
is the condition of oneness the Lord wants us to have in our
marriage relationship. It is the ideal. But it may not always be that
way. We will represent disharmony in the marriage by placing an
"X" through the line, indicating an absence of unity in that
marriage.

When lack of unity exists in a marriage, an independent party
is sometimes invited to meet with the marriage partners to help
resolve differences and relieve strained relationships. Many
marriage counselors, psychologists, and other experts spend a
great amount of time and energy trying to help marriage partners
reconcile their differences, eliminate offensive behavior, or
compromise expectations in order to defuse volatile conditions.
They might identify many contributing causes, such as lack of

communication, financial irresponsibility, religious differences, in-law interference, and so on. Sometimes people are able to make adjustments and calm troubled waters. But that is a process of treating symptoms rather than the single most serious problem.

Remember when the Savior directed us to be one, he added, "if ye are not one, ye are not mine" (D&C 38:27). The first part of the statement, "if ye are not one," identifies the problem: a lack of unity with one another. But the second part, "ye are not mine," is the reason for the problem. When we live in a state of disharmony with each other, that problem is a consequence of our failing to first establish a state of unity with the Lord. **If we are not one with each other, it is** *because* **we are not one with the Lord.** We are not His. Our ability to achieve unity with one another on a horizontal level is dependent upon our first establishing a oneness with the Lord, which is a vertical dimension.

Picture the graphic again. In addition to having a horizontal line between the two people, visualize a diagonal vertical line connecting each individual to the Lord above, forming a triangle that connects the three personages. If there is an "X" through the line between the two spouses, there will always be an "X" through the vertical line between the Lord and one or both of the spouses.

If a marriage relationship is in a state of disharmony, wise are the spouses who follow the pattern of the Apostles who were with the Savior at the Last Supper. When He stated that one of them would be His betrayer, they did not look to any of the others present as the possible one. Rather, they each asked, "Is it I?" (Mark 14:19). Rather than point an accusing finger at a spouse, each of us should first examine ourselves to find if we might be failing to represent the Savior's way or nature, thus betraying Him and our covenant relationship with Him.

Let's suppose that one spouse is in harmony with the Lord, is reflecting a Christ-like life, and is behaving as the Lord would have him/her behave. If there is still an "X" on the horizontal line, then it would be clear where the problem is and whose life needs a course correction. Effort could then be made to seek kindly and lovingly to help the companion make adjustments as necessary to establish harmony or unity between the spouse and the Lord. There may also be a need to enlist the assistance of priesthood leaders or utilize other resources, but there would be a far greater chance of successfully obtaining a state of oneness when there is a correct identification of the real source of problems. When two people are living in harmony with the Lord's will, they will also be united in their relationship with each other.

Let's take another example: this time, the two people are a father and his son. Sometimes a parent and child do not see eye to eye and do not agree on what is right or good on various issues. Occasionally, we hear a phrase used to identify the cause of such problems as a "generation gap." That phrase is used by some to justify a lack of resolution effort and is used as an excuse for just waiting out the issue until the passage of time might solve it. But again, the real problem in a lack of oneness is a lack of unity between the Lord and one or both of the people involved. If there is an "X" through the horizontal line, there will also be an "X" through one or both of the vertical lines. Maybe the father is impatient or even abusive, or maybe he does not listen to or spend time with his children, or maybe he lacks understanding of what the gospel teaches him he should do. Perhaps a wise bishop will be able to counsel and help the father correct his failings and weaknesses.

But after these efforts, what if there is still an "X" through the line between him and his son? If so, the dad now knows the problem is really between the son and the Lord. And how does that knowledge benefit the father? The son may exhibit his problem in the way he speaks and acts inappropriately against his father. But those are only symptoms of his rebellion towards the Lord. Having this knowledge, the father does not react personally towards the boy, but takes a course that could assist his son to either create or strengthen a proper relationship with the Lord. As an example, suppose the father is requiring the son to hold to the Lord's dating standard of age sixteen, and the son vehemently objects. The father may wonder if he should yield to the son's objection. If he does so, he takes himself out of harmony with the Lord, and nothing is resolved in the Lord's way. But when the father knows he is properly representing the will of the Lord, it becomes an appropriate objective to help the son realize he is not resisting his father, but rather is in opposition to the Lord.

Nephi recorded a father-son situation: "I beheld my brethren, and they were disputing one with another concerning the things which my father had spoken unto them" (1 Ne. 15:2). Their relationship with their father did not have unity. Nephi went on to say that his father "truly spake many great things unto them, which were hard to be understood, save a man should inquire of the Lord." But the brothers "did not look unto the Lord as they ought" (1 Ne. 15:3). What was the source of the great things of which Lehi spoke? Lehi was speaking about the things he had received from the Lord. But the brothers went on to say, "We cannot understand the words which our father hath spoken." Nephi then asked, "Have ye inquired of the Lord? And they said . . . we have not; for the Lord maketh no such thing known unto us" (1 Ne. 15:7–9).

The brothers were at variance with their father. There was an "X" through the line between them. But when Lehi was representing the

Lord in the things he spoke, the vertical line between him and the Lord was solid. So where was the problem? The sons did not look to the Lord for assurance and instruction. They did not communicate with Him and so failed to understand what their father had already received from the Lord. There was an "X" through the line between the sons and the Lord. So Nephi wisely recalled what the Lord had said unto them: "If ye will not harden your hearts, and ask me in faith, believing that ye shall receive, with diligence in keeping my commandments, surely these things shall be made known unto you" (1 Ne. 15:11).

It is not difficult to imagine Nephi speaking to his brothers and saying, "You can understand the same thing our dad is talking about, but you have to put your life in order first. Your problem is not with our father; he is all right. He does not have to worry about what he is telling you, because he knows where it is coming from. But you have the problem. You do not go to the Lord, you do not want to know if our father is right, and furthermore, you really do not want him to be right." Interestingly, Nephi did not encourage his brothers to listen to their dad. He maintained that their problem was with the Lord and attempted to persuade them to unite with Him. We note that Nephi and his father got along with each other very well. But it was not just based on a father-and-son relationship. It was based on both of these great souls seeking to know and act upon the will of the Lord. There was power in that unity.

Even when Nephi broke his bow and his father murmured against the Lord, Nephi did not attempt to correct or chasten Lehi; that was not his role or stewardship. He knew Lehi's problem was a vertical one. So he made a new bow, then went to his father and asked where he should go to obtain food. Nephi knew full well his dad did not know the answer to the question, and would not know unless he received it from the Lord. But first, he would have to humble himself, repent, and, with the help of the Lord, repair the damage. He did so and was then able to receive needed directions and continue to nurture a spiritual oneness with the Lord (see 1 Ne. 16:18–26).

The Lord has structured the organization of His church for the very purpose of helping all of us be unified as a people. The Apostle Paul taught that the Lord

> gave some, apostles; and some, prophets; and some, evangelists; and some, pastors and teachers [priesthood leaders];
>
> For the perfecting of the saints, for the work of the ministry, for the edifying of the body of Christ:
>
> *Till we all come in the unity of the faith,* and of the knowledge of the Son of God, unto a perfect man, unto the measure of the stature of the fulness of Christ (Eph. 4:11–13; emphasis added).

Each of us would do well to remember the role of the Lord's priesthood leaders. They are accountable to Him to learn and reflect His will to the people. They are responsible to act in His behalf and be united with Him in teaching and ministering in His kingdom. Theirs is the responsibility to bring the people to the Lord that they might be purified and perfected through Him. As the leaders are united with the Lord, so also are the people able to be united with Him and with each other when they follow the teachings and principles presented by His leaders. We ought to refrain from criticizing or "second guessing" the Lord's leadership. If they are united with the Lord, we want to be united with them. If they need correction, it is the Lord's responsibility to do it, not ours. We must maintain our own spiritual unity with Him, which is violated and diminished if we step into the relationship between the Lord and those who are called to represent Him.

The Lord taught this principle as it applies to Church members and the First Presidency of the Church. He said, "Whosoever receiveth my word receiveth me, and whosoever receiveth me, receiveth those, the First Presidency, whom I have sent, whom I have made counselors for my name's sake unto you" (D&C 112:20). A few years later, He emphasized that relationship with a powerful promise for those who honor and embrace it. He said:

> And if my people will hearken unto my voice, and unto the voice of my servants [First Presidency] whom I have appointed to lead my people, behold, verily I say unto you, *they shall not be moved out of their place.*
>
> But if they will not hearken to my voice, nor unto the voice of those men whom I have appointed, they shall not be blest, because they pollute mine holy grounds, and mine holy ordinances, and charters, and my holy words which I give unto them (D&C 124: 45–46; emphasis added).

The Lord illustrated the gravity of failing to follow His appointed leaders by describing the actions of a brother by the name of Almon Babbit: "And with my servant Almon Babbitt, there are many things with which I am not pleased; behold, he aspireth to establish his counsel instead of the counsel which I have ordained, even that of the Presidency of my Church; and he setteth up a golden calf for the worship of my people" (D&C 124:84).

When any of us determine that our wisdom and judgment is more favorable to follow than that of the Lord whose guidance and counsel comes to us through His priesthood leaders, we are following the folly of Almon Babbit. We are out of harmony with the Lord, whose principles and practices we have ignored and thus are not united with his servants, the First Presidency. It is tantamount to setting up a golden calf as an object of our worship in exchange for the Savior whom we worship, the Lord of us all upon whom we depend for our salvation and eternal lives. May we instead seek to live in response to Lehi's plea to his sons when he said, ". . . arise from the dust, my sons, and be men, and be determined in one mind and in one heart, united in all things, that ye may not come down into captivity" (2 Ne. 1:21).

We have talked about two dimensions of unity, which we described as being horizontal and vertical. There is a third that is closely related to the other two that we will call *internal.* This concept refers to the congruity or lack thereof between the standards or values a person embraces and his quality of character or his actual internal nature. In other words, is he what he has outwardly committed to be or what he represents himself to be? If the answer is yes, then he possesses an internal oneness with self. There is no gap that waits to be closed for him to have personal peace.

The Lord declared the standard that His people should observe and apply in their lives. He said, "And even so I have sent mine everlasting covenant [the fulness of the gospel and its covenants] into the world, to be a light to the world, and to be *a standard for my people,* and for the Gentiles to seek to it, and to be a messenger before my face to prepare the way before me" (D&C 45:9; emphasis added).

The question for each of us is, "Are we living the standard we have made covenants to keep, or is there a gap we need to close?" Some people become frustrated with their failure to be what they should and want to be. We observe three different processes people pursue to eliminate the difference between the standard and themselves.

First, some mentally lower the standard and determine what they think the standard ought to be. Or they rationalize that the higher standard taught by Church authorities is not appropriate for them or perhaps doesn't matter. Then their conduct is not different than the standard they have perceived should be observed, and for the present time, they are content. **This is called unrighteous rationalization.** The Lord said, "Unto every kingdom is given a law; and unto every law there are certain bounds also and conditions. All beings who abide not in those conditions *are not justified*" (D&C 88:38–39; emphasis added).

Second, some make conscious efforts to appear to be observing the standard, when in reality their actual nature is not what they would have others believe about them. For example, they may be kind and loving people publicly, but perhaps are impatient, mean-spirited, cruel, or maybe even physically abusive in more private settings. Still others may appear to be spiritual people outwardly, but may be hiding an addiction to pornography or some other evil practice. **This is called hypocrisy.** The Lord said, "Thou shalt not do as the hypocrites" (3 Ne. 13:5). The Lord further described the destiny of hypocrites as follows: "He that saith he receiveth it [my law] and doeth it not, the same is not my disciple, and shall be cast out from among you" (D&C 41:5).

Third, the Lord's way is to leave the standards as He revealed them and teach the people to be obedient. When deviations occur, the individual should repent and make changes as necessary to internally be in harmony with gospel requirements and the Spirit of the Lord. President Ezra Taft Benson suggested a marvelous way we can achieve such a condition. He said, "Every Latter-day Saint should make the study of this book [Book of Mormon] a lifetime pursuit. Otherwise he is placing his soul in jeopardy and neglecting that which could give spiritual and intellectual unity to his whole life" (CR, Apr. 1975, 97).

Many have asked, "How obedient does the Lord expect us to be? How exact and precise must we be in reflecting His teachings and standards? What if we try our best and still don't completely fulfill our assignments?" We will let the Lord answer those questions. He declared:

> Verily, verily, I say unto you, that when I give a commandment to any of the sons of men to do a work unto my name, and those sons of men go with all their might and with all they have to perform that work, and cease not their diligence, and their enemies come upon them and hinder them from performing that work, behold, it behooveth me to require that work no more at the hands of those sons of men, but to *accept of their offerings* (D&C 124:49; emphasis added).

The true measure of success in life, of knowing one has reached the desired level of unity with the Lord, is to be accepted of Him. How we can know of that acceptance is further described by the Lord when He said that the gifts of the Holy Spirit "are given for the benefit of those who love me and keep all my commandments, *and him that seeketh so to do*" (D&C 46:9; emphasis added). Those who know they are earnestly striving and seeking to keep the Lord's commandments can be assured they are united with the Lord in what He expects and accepts from each of us.

In very simple terms, we see that the law of unity is a fulfilling representation of the Lord's answer to the question: "Master, which is the great commandment in the Law? Jesus said unto him, Thou shalt love the Lord thy God with all thy heart, and with all thy soul, and with all thy mind. This is the first and great commandment. And the second is like unto it, Thou shalt love thy neighbour as thyself. On these two commandments hang all the law and the prophets" (Matt. 22:36–40).

First, we are to love the Lord and be one with Him, vertically. Second, we must love our neighbor and be one with him, horizontally. Third, we are to love self and have unity with the Lord's gospel and His Spirit, internally. This is precisely what the Lord prayed for when He asked that His disciples be one, the same as the Savior and His Father are one with each other. The line defining their relationship is solid, without any absence of unity. For us to be one with each other, we must first be one with the Lord; and to have both of those relationships solid, we must develop and nurture an internal makeup that reflects the true nature of a disciple of Christ. Unity in all three dimensions results in power.

President George Q. Cannon said,

The distinguishing feature of the religion taught by Jesus was that it would make His followers one; and He gave this as one of the evidences by which the world might know it was true.

When men receive this Gospel, wherever they may be, however widely separated they may be, as soon as they are confirmed members of the Church, they receive a spirit that fills them with that union, and when they are brought together from the ends of the earth, they feel alike and are drawn together. . . . [This unity] comes from God. It is the power that reigns in heaven. It is the power that makes heaven the glorious place that it is described to be.

If we were not united, we would not be the people of God. It is the true sign by which the people of God may be found. . . . (*Gospel Truth*, 202–03, 210).

President Heber C. Kimball declared, "*Power dwells in unity, not in discord; in humility, not pride; in sacrifice, not selfishness; obedience, not rebellion*" (*Life of Heber C. Kimball*, 64; emphasis added).

Where there is unity in the Church and in our families, there is Zion and a pure people, blessed with power from on high.

CONCLUSION

As we noted in chapter one, when the Saints were asked to gather in Ohio, the Lord promised them an endowment of power from on high. When Joseph Smith received the revelation commanding the Saints to build a house unto the Lord in Kirtland, he sent a copy of it to William W. Phelps in Missouri, along with an accompanying letter addressed to Brother Phelps, containing the following excerpts:

> I send you the "olive leaf" [D&C Section 88] which we have plucked from the Tree of Paradise, the Lord's message of peace to us . . . You will see that the Lord commanded us, in Kirtland, to build a house of God, and establish a school for the Prophets, this is the word of the Lord to us, and we must, yea, the Lord helping us, we will obey: as on conditions of our obedience He has promised us great things; yea, even a visit from the heavens to honor us with His own presence. We greatly fear before the Lord lest we should fail of this great honor, which our Master proposes to confer on us; we are seeking for humility and great faith lest we be ashamed in His presence (*HC,* 1:316–17).

The Lord kept His promise on April 3, 1836, just a few days after the dedication of the Kirtland Temple, making that day one of the most significant days in the history of the Church. Of the spiritual events of that day, Joseph wrote, "We saw the Lord standing upon the breastwork of the pulpit, before us; and under his feet was a paved work of pure gold, in color like amber" (D&C 110:2). As the Savior spoke to the two brethren (Joseph Smith and Oliver Cowdery), He identified Himself as Jehovah who was slain, was resurrected, and who lives today (see D&C 110:4). In that brief introductory encounter we have been given another witness from the Savior Himself as to the reality of His Atonement and Resurrection. We also have two mortal witnesses who saw Him and heard His divine declaration, "I am he who liveth" (D&C 110:4).

Following the Savior's appearance, Moses restored the keys of the gathering of Israel from the four parts of the earth (see D&C 110:11). All those who have been gathered into the kingdom of God throughout the countries of the world are recipients of the blessings that have resulted from the restoration of the keys of gathering.

Elias also appeared and restored keys. Who is Elias and what did he restore? Elias is Noah (see Joseph Fielding Smith, CR, Apr. 1960, 72). He restored the keys of the dispensation in which Abraham lived (see D&C 110:12). Therefore, all of the blessings promised to Abraham are now available to everyone who seeks to obtain the ordinances in the temple. These blessings include eternal marriage vows with promises of eternal posterity and family relationships through the patriarchal order of the priesthood. Multitudes of Father's children have been recipients of these blessings that have flowed from that house in Kirtland.

Elijah also restored priesthood keys (see D&C 110:13–16). As to the nature of those keys, Elder Joseph Fielding Smith has taught: "Elijah restored to this Church and, if they would receive it, to the world, the keys of the sealing power; and that sealing power puts the stamp of approval upon every ordinance that is done in this Church and more particularly those that are performed in the temples of the Lord" (CR, Apr. 1948, 135).

Every person and every family, both living and dead, who have received ordinances of the priesthood can be assured that the power to keep those ordinances intact throughout all eternity was restored in the Kirtland Temple. The blessings that have flowed from that temple have given literally millions of people great cause to rejoice. The fame of that house is now known throughout foreign lands. The endowed powers and authority from on high that were restored in that temple are presently being utilized and manifested in temples of the Lord in the various nations of the earth. (See Otten and Caldwell, *Sacred Truths of the Doctrine and Covenants,* 2:248–49.)

ENDOWED WITH THE PRESENCE OF GOD

The bestowal of the various endowments of power appear to be of such vital significance that both God the Father and His Son graced many of the events with their presence. Their appearance served as a heavenly endorsement of the experiences that were taking place in fulfillment of the promise of an endowment of power from on high.

Brother Karl R. Anderson also identifies a number of times when the Savior appeared during this Kirtland period, and he documents four separate sites where the Father and the Son appeared (see *Joseph Smith's Kirtland,* 107–13).

1. Joseph Smith, Lyman Wight, and Harvey Whitlock saw the Father and the Son in the log schoolhouse on the Isaac Morley farm during a conference held June 3–6, 1831.

2. Joseph Smith and Sidney Rigdon beheld the Father and the Son in a vision received February 16, 1832, in an upper room of the John Johnson home in Hiram, Ohio. (See D&C 76:20.)

3. The Father and the Son were seen by many of the brethren when each appeared in the Newel K. Whitney store in March 1833 at the time of the organization of the First Presidency.

4. On January 21, 1836, Joseph Smith was in the Kirtland Temple and saw the celestial kingdom, including the blazing throne of God, whereon was seated the Father and the Son. (See D&C 137:3.)

Perhaps most of us have not yet caught the magnitude of the impact or glimpsed the importance of the events connected with the restoration of all things in this last gospel dispensation. Righteous people and prophets from the days of Adam to the present have anticipated and looked forward to this period of the earth's history. After all, the Savior's millennial reign is waiting in the wings to be ushered onto the world's stage of life. These last days are filled with an abundance of opportunity for the Lord's people to obtain heavenly spiritual power, enabling them to recognize and resist influences of evil and acquire peace in the presence of the Lord's Spirit.

After reviewing some of the marvelous restoration events and mentioning some of the noble prophets of the past who came to restore priesthood keys and powers associated with their respective dispensations, the Prophet Joseph Smith exclaimed:

Brethren, shall we not go on in so great a cause? Go forward and not backward. Courage, brethren; and on, on to the victory! Let your hearts rejoice, and be exceedingly glad. Let the earth break forth into singing. . . .

Let the mountains shout for joy, and all ye valleys cry aloud; and all ye seas and dry lands tell the wonders of your Eternal King! And ye rivers, and brooks, and rills, flow down with gladness. Let the woods and all the trees of the field praise the Lord; and ye solid rocks weep for joy! And let the sun, moon, and the morning stars sing together, and let all the sons of God shout for joy! And let the eternal creations declare his name forever and ever! And again I say, how glorious is the voice we hear from heaven, proclaiming in our ears, glory, and salvation, and honor, and immortality, and eternal life; kingdoms, principalities, and powers!

Behold, the great day of the Lord is at hand (D&C 128:22–24).

The rise of the Church and the rolling forth of the Kingdom of God is truly the greatest cause on the earth today. May each of us "go on **in** so great a cause" and not just be aware of the process as observers or spectators only. Speaking of the power and destiny of the Church as an institution, President Gordon B. Hinckley declared:

This Church is true. It will weather every storm that beats against it. It will outlast every critic who rises to mock it. It was established by God our Eternal Father for the blessing of His sons and daughters of all generations. It carries the name of Him who stands as its head, even the Lord Jesus Christ, the Savior of the world. It is governed and moves by the power of the priesthood. It sends forth to the world another witness of the divinity of the Lord ("Keep the Faith," *Ensign*, Sept. 1985, 6).

It would be interesting to modify President Hinckley's declaration a little by replacing the words referring to the Church with words that have reference to *individuals* in the Church who have been endowed with power from on high. The truths he proclaimed can be the same in both instances:

> This person is true. He will weather every storm that beats against him. He will outlast every critic who rises to mock him. He was created by God our Eternal Father for the blessing of His sons and daughters of all generations. He carries the name of Him who stands as his head, even the Lord Jesus Christ, the Savior of the world. He is governed and moves by the power of the priesthood. He goes forth to the world as another witness of the divinity of the Lord ("Keep the Faith," *Ensign*, Sept. 1985, 6; modified version).

The person described above is not a rare or unique individual in the Church. There are many members of the Church who have the power that enables them to be true to their covenants. In a vision provided by an angel of the Lord, Nephi of old described the Lord's people in these latter days:

> I, Nephi, beheld the power of the Lamb of God, that it descended upon the saints of the church of the Lamb, and upon the covenant people of the Lord, who were scattered upon all the face of the earth; and they were armed with righteousness and with the power of God in great glory (1 Ne. 14:14).

When the Lord's church was organized in this dispensation, the Savior revealed that He gave Joseph Smith "power from on high" that he might fulfill the Lord's purposes and accomplish His marvelous work. (See D&C 20:8.) Just as Joseph Smith needed power from heavenly sources, so also are we dependent upon that same power in order to fulfill the Lord's expectations of us, be accepted of Him, and be welcomed back into His presence. May this condition be the lot of each of us. It can and will be if we seek for, obtain, and retain POWER FROM ON HIGH.

BIBLIOGRAPHY

BOOKS

Anderson, Karl R. *Joseph Smith's Kirtland.* Salt Lake City: Deseret Book, 1989.

Benson, Ezra Taft. *A Witness and a Warning.* Salt Lake City: Deseret Book, 1988.

Cannon, George Q. *Gospel Truth.* Vol. 1. Comp. Jerreld L. Newquist. Salt Lake City: Zion's Book Store, 1957.

———. *Gospel Truth,* Vol. 2. Salt Lake City: Deseret Book, 1974.

Clark, J. Reuben, Jr. *Behold the Lamb of God.* Salt Lake City: Deseret Book, 1962.

———. *Man—God's Greatest Miracle.* Salt Lake City: Deseret Book, 1956.

Cook, Roy J., ed. *One Hundred and One Famous Poems.* Chicago: The Cable Company, 1929.

Doxey, Roy W. *The Latter-day Prophets and the Doctrine and Covenants.* 4 Vols. Salt Lake City: Deseret Book, 1965.

Ehat, Andrew, and Lyndon W. Cook. *The Words of Joseph Smith.* Salt Lake City: Bookcraft, 1980.

Featherstone, Vaughn J. *The Disciple of Christ.* Salt Lake City: Deseret Book, 1984.

———. *The Incomparable Christ.* Salt Lake City: Deseret Book, 1995.

Grant, Heber J. *Gospel Standards.* Comp. G. Homer Durham. Salt Lake City: Deseret News Press, 1969.

Jenson, Andrew. *LDS Biographical Encyclopedia.* 4 Vols. Salt Lake City: Publishers Press, 1971.

Journal of Discourses. 26 vols. London: Latter-day Saints' Book Depot, 1854–86.

Kimball, Spencer W. *The Teachings of Spencer W. Kimball.* Ed. Edward L. Kimball. Salt Lake City: Bookcraft, 1982.

———. *Faith Precedes the Miracle.* Salt Lake City: Deseret Book, 1972.

———. *The Miracle of Forgiveness.* Salt Lake City: Bookcraft, 1969.

Lectures on Faith. American Fork, Utah: Covenant Communications, 2005.

Lee, Harold B. *From the Valley of Despair to the Mountain Peaks of Hope.* Salt Lake City: Deseret News Press, 1971.

Ludlow, Daniel H., comp. *Latter-day Prophets Speak.* Salt Lake City: Bookcraft, 1948.

Maxwell, Neal A. *Moving in His Majesty and Power.* Salt Lake City: Deseret Book, 2004.

McConkie, Bruce R. *Doctrinal New Testament Commentary.* 3 Vols. Salt Lake City: Bookcraft, 1970.

———. *Mormon Doctrine.* Salt Lake City: Bookcraft, 1958.

McKay, David O. *Stepping Stones to an Abundant Life.* Salt Lake City: Deseret Book, 1971

———. *Treasures of Life.* Salt Lake City: Deseret Book, 1970.

Nuttall, John. *Journal, Dec. 1876–Mar. 1884.* Salt Lake City: Calvin P. Rudd Library.

Otten, Leaun G., and C. Max Caldwell. *Sacred Truths of the Doctrine and Covenants.* 2 Vols. Salt Lake City: Deseret Book, 1983.

Our Heritage: A Brief History of The Church of Jesus Christ of Latter-day Saints. Salt Lake City: The Church of Jesus Christ of Latter-day Saints, 1996.

Shelley, Harry Rowe, "The King of Love My Shepherd Is," *Sing Unto God.* Minneapolis, Minnesota: Schmitt Music Centers, 1952. 58–63.

Smith, Joseph F. *Gospel Doctrine.* Salt Lake City: Deseret Book, 1956.

Smith, Joseph Fielding, comp. *Teachings of the Prophet Joseph Smith.* Salt Lake City: Deseret Book, 1963.

———. *Doctrines of Salvation.* 3 Vols. Salt Lake City: Bookcraft, 1955.

Smith, Hyrum M. *Doctrine and Covenants Commentary.* Salt Lake City: Deseret Book, 1950.

Smith, Joseph. *History of The Church of Jesus Christ of Latter-day Saints.* 2nd ed., 7 Vols. Salt Lake City: Deseret Book, 1959.

Smith, Joseph. *Joseph Smith Translation of the Holy Bible.* Independence, Missouri: Herald Publishing House, 1964.

St. Francis of Assisi. *Interreligious Insight.* Jan 2004 edition.

Talmage, James E. *Jesus the Christ.* Salt Lake City: Deseret Book, 1951.

———. *The House of the Lord.* Salt Lake City: Bookcraft, 1962.

Tullidge, Edward W. *The Women of Mormondom.* 3rd reprint. Salt Lake City: Lithographic Reprint, 1973.

Watson, Elden J. *Manuscript History of Brigham Young, 1846–1847.* Salt Lake City: Elden J. Watson, 1971.

Whitney, Orson F. *Life of Heber C. Kimball.* Salt Lake City: Bookcraft, 1945.

Woodruff, Wilford. *The Discourses of Wilford Woodruff.* Ed. G. Homer Durham. Salt Lake City: Bookcraft, 1946.

PERIODICALS AND PAMPHLETS

Ballard, Melvin J. *The Three Degrees of Glory.* Salt Lake City: Deseret Book, 1922.

Church News. Salt Lake City: Deseret News.

Conference Report. Salt Lake City: The Church of Jesus Christ of Latter-day Saints.

Ensign. Salt Lake City: The Church of Jesus Christ of Latter-day Saints.

Improvement Era. Salt Lake City: The Church of Jesus Christ of Latter-day Saints.

Millennial Star. Manchester, England: The Church of Jesus Christ of Latter-day Saints.

Relief Society Magazine. Salt Lake City: The Church of Jesus Christ of Latter-day Saints, Feb. 1968.

Smith, Joseph Fielding. *Church History and Modern Revelation.* 4 vols. Salt Lake City: Deseret News Press, 1946.

The Instructor. Salt Lake City: The Church of Jesus Christ of Latter-day Saints.

INDEX